I AIN'T HAVIN

CHAPTER 1

I was eighteen and had not long finished college, I did want to join the police force but I just couldn't decide so I chose to first try working for a security company based in Rochester Kent.

The company was average, they used to give me lifts to some sites and take me home, the cons was I was paid less for being female.

Over the first few months I enjoyed it and I got to be a dog handler at a posh school end of year ball in Rochester, I spent the shift walking this really cute German shepherd around, and I got some great compliments from the ball organiser at the end of the shift.

My supervisor Nick was ok to start with then after a few months he started getting very flirty, Nick was around mid-thirties, quite short for a guy and had a massive beer belly, I did make it clear to him that I wasn't interested and that I was already in a relationship but he still continued with his over the top flirting.

Being eighteen I was quite shy and nervous and I would never stick up for myself so I just used to laugh off his advances.

Out of the blue I received a text from his work phone saying ' would you have a relationship with me based on sex?', I ignored it and deleted the text as my partner at the time was very possessive and would of gone mad at reading that text.

One night he gave me a lift home from a work site , we was chatting and he kept saying " you know we can stop at a layby", I was so shocked I didn't say anything, I started to get a bit scared as he kept repeating " you're not home yet I might still stop at a layby", I was so glad when I finally got home but within in a few minutes of getting in I got a text from him saying ' I love you' I was now really freaking out about it .

I hadn't being working for the company very long and Nick had been there for a few years so I didn't know what to do but finally I went into the office and spoke to Sammy the manager and told him what had happened and that I wanted It to stop.

It was quite brave of me to bring this up as normally I would be too worried to say anything, he seemed nice but said I most likely took it the wrong way but he said he was going to allow me to work at a site that I could get to and from without needing lifts from Nick.

I thought everything was sorted, they sent me to a packaging factory in Hythe, I would be there from six at night till six in the morning, A Very easy job sitting in a reception desk after all the staff went home.

I would do hourly patrols and could spend the rest of my time reading. I remember reading a book all about Kenneth Williams's life, a very interesting read.

I worked two shifts there then I was dismissed from the company (obviously to do with my complaint) , they had tried to say I had made a mess at the site and had spilt a whole two litre bottle of coke from the toilets to the reception desk, saying the carpets had to be cleaned, well I know the floors was all marble and I never drunk coke , I couldn't believe they had made something like this up and they was going to charge me two hundred pounds out of my wages for the clean up (what con-artists).

I was so upset and told my mum everything , my mum called the boss and gave him a right ear full and told him he will not be taking any money out of my wages or she would help me take them to court for sexual harassment, and guess what I got paid in full.

Being how sensitive I was I stayed away from security for a few months and joined Tesco as an assistant.

Sometime later I spotted a job for a door supervisor at a dog racing track advertised at the job centre, I spoke to the security manager who offered me a paid trial shift on the Saturday night.

Saturday night came and I was quite nervous, I met up with the manager who said straight away "sorry I can't offer you a job I'm concerned about your size", to be fair I'm five foot five and a size twelve not a huge burly doorman that you would normally see, he continued "but I offered you a trial shift so I will still pay you for tonight ", not a great start and I was a bit gutted.

I was working there with a guy called Steve he also worked in the prison service, it was a nice place and I had never been there before, they had dog racing in the day time, dinner table service and in the evening there was music, dance floor and club area only for the guests that was already there, there was no entry after eight at night for outsiders.. Thankfully I got to prove myself that night.

Steve and I was standing on the front door when a young male aged around eighteen came to the door , I could tell that he was angry about something, we refused him entry , he demanded to be let in and told us why, that him and his girlfriend had split up and she worked there behind the bar upstairs, he was so desperate to see her and was getting more angry with us , I managed to get him to listen to me and said I understood why he wanted to see her but if he did she would most likely not be happy that he had come to her place of work and caused a scene, he understood and calmed down, thanked me and left, this impressed Steve and he said he would talk to our manager Jason .

Jason called me the next day and said Steve had been singing my praises and said he was sorry for doubting me and offered me every Friday and Saturday there which I happily accepted.

The team grew to about four door staff, two on the front door and two inside and we would rotate every so often , I remember standing there watching the crowd on the dance floor with the girls aloud song ' sounds of the underground' playing feeling really proud of this job.

Not a lot happened there , there was a few kick offs , five guys stormed the front door after being refused entry and one of them got to the top of the stairs while we was trying to get the others out of the door , the guy was quite drunk, he must of missed the steps and came crashing back down, landing with his jaw out right , I heard a crunch and thought he had broken his neck but probably due to his intoxication he was fine and we managed to make them all leave.

I think I met Anne Robinson there, she looked and sounded like her, we got chatting , she was really nice and I asked if she was her but she kept laughing and avoiding the question, when she left she said goodbye and as she walked away she did the Anne Robinson 'wink' at me ,, so who knows!

I then got a part-time job at a shopping store as a security officer , I worked two days in the week and on Sundays , there was a female security manager , she was really nice and was quite impressed that I was a female working on the doors, I liked it there but it was hard work .

 The security manager would tell me to stand at the front of the store , then a senior store manager would come to me and tell me to put sandwiches out at the front of the store (he out ranked my manager so I had to do it) then the security manager would have a go at me for putting out the sandwiches , I got pissed off with this and went to the deputy store manager who confirmed I had to do what the senior manager wanted, my contract wasn't as a security officer but a general assistant so I had to do what others asked , still I got on really well with the security manager , we had a right laugh chasing shop lifters, the one I remembered was someone ran out with a TV , we chased him and he turn around and throw the TV at us , it hit the ground but a manager still put it back on the shelves , I was sad when my security manager left , a guy replaced her and he was such a moody guy and would get annoyed if anyone made him leave his office , sometime later a female member of staff on the clothing department confined in me that clothes was going out the back door during the night, meaning being stolen by staff , she didn't want to go to any manager about it but asked if I could do something about it , I thought the best thing to do was go to a union rep , but my mistake, What I didn't know was the union reps husband worked nights and from what went on after it seemed he may be in on it , I started to get pushed out , I would be called into the office to be informed that customers would ring the store making complaints about me , one which was shocking , a customer had stated they saw me carrying a knife on my belt ..wtf, then night staff made a complaint that when I finished working on the doors I would pop in to get some shopping now and then, some staff said I would go out the back in the warehouse, unfortunately there was no cctv to prove otherwise , the last straw was the union reps husband had said I had threatened him , I had enough and quit.

I spent a few months at the racing track which I did enjoy but not much ever happened there and I wanted something more challenging, the staff there were lovely and would cook us a roast every Saturday before our shift started.

I then found a door job with more hours just outside of the town where my mother lived in Rainham, a nice little pub or so I thought, so me and a friend called Tony went and worked there with a guy called Ian who told us it was a very rough place and he would be leaving soon.

We worked with Ian for a few weeks and it wasn't to bad, a few drunks asked to leave and others told to behave that kind of thing... then Ian handed in his notice, I got a call from the security manager asking me to run the contract for him and supply the staff and give out wages, I had no problem with that, we did the work and was always paid on time, there was never a problem, but the pub was a different story. We couldn't seem to get the right door staff for the pub, this pub was what you would call a regulars pub, and you needed some rapport with them.

We got a guy we knew who already worked the doors called "big Steve" and he was big, imagine the big guy from the film 'the green mile' just not as tall , he was awesome and such a lovely guy, only problem was his social skills at work . He's first shift was on my night off, I came back to find the pub manager Ron wasn't happy with Steve.

See Steve was more of an old school doorman, he was great in fights but that was it, regulars had tried speaking to him and he just grunted at them and refused to shake peoples hands at the end of the night... unfortunately Ron didn't want him back, I felt crap about it there's me in my early twenties telling a guy in his thirties that he wasn't allowed back but he was a laid back guy and took it well.

The next guy to work with us I met in passing called Tim, he was a jiu jitsu instructor so I thought awesome he will be really good. Until we had a major kick off inside and Tim had got a guy in a head lock and they was just spinning around like some buckaroo game so little me went over to help him restrain the guy. Again management saw it and didn't want him back.

We finally managed to get some good guys that lasted... I can't remember how I met them but along came Shane and Paul... we finally had a good lasting team and boy did we need it.

We had a massive fight between two local gangs, one of the gangs drove there bmw car at us and I had to throw myself out of the way, falling into a brick wall scraping my back.

We also had a knife attack , a guy was running around trying to stab this blonde guy in the car park ,

He tried to escape by jumping into his convertible car, the guy then tried to stab the tyres on the car which didn't work, I looked over the road and saw a police car sat at the traffic lights, I ran over and explained what was happening and they turned around and drove into the car park, I saw the guy with the knife head over to a little mini car that two girls was sat in, I had a feeling he was going to drop the knife in the car which I relayed to the police , but they let the car go and searched the guy and what a shocker no knife so he was sent on his smug way.

The pub was a real learning curve for me , a eye opener and we had to be alert all the time , I only got assaulted once thankfully, we had a kick off inside and I restrained a guy when another guy blindsided me and smacked me in the face.. it didn't hurt too much , Tony also got hit once, we had asked a young male to leave for intoxication , he wouldn't move from the front door and kept arguing with Tony , Tony held the door partly open to speak to the guy , I don't know how I knew I guess it was just a feeling but I knew the guy was going to kick off, I kept asking Tony to let go of the door so I could stand with him , he didn't listen to me then all of a sudden the guy punches Tony in the face, Tony let go of the door and I grabbed the male and put him on the floor then Shane and Paul helped restrain him , the males mood changed while we was waiting for the police and he started crying and calling out 'mum' and pissed himself , he was arrested .

We had a big issue one night which was something I really learnt from.

One of the barmaids had broken up with her boyfriend and he turned up drunk, high on cocaine and very angry , we turned him away but he managed to get in through a unlocked back staff door , I went to restrain him and bent his wrist to inflict pain to get him to submit but he felt nothing he was like a wild animal , the four of us managed to just grab him and get him out the front , he was going mental, kicking the front door then he went round the side , this pub had windows everywhere he was banging and looking for things to throw , I quickly moved the punters away from the windows, the police turned up and it took eight officers to get him into the van , he came back the following week to apologise for his behaviour, he showed us the palm of his hand and there was a big mark where he had had to have a operation to correct a nerve that had been damaged by resisting arrest with the police. his problem was he was a big user of cocaine and alcohol.

A customer I always remember from there was a regular called " richy rich ", he wasn't rich but I think he got the nickname as he was always buying everyone drinks , he was a lovely guy , never caused trouble and always respectful.

We had a big kick off one night and somehow he got hurt, most likely from trying to stop the fight, he ended up with a hole in his cheek the size of a twenty pence piece.

The police officers that arrived was complete assholes, the female officer was so rude to me when I was trying to tell her what had happened but she kept snapping at me but as I was so young and unconfident in myself I just allowed it, but it did start making me dislike the police a bit.

Months went by and I was enjoying working the four shifts and getting stuck in there , one weekend Shane pointed two guys out and said to me " I think they are undercover old bill" , he went on to explain he had seen them every weekend for the last month they would come in and order two non alcoholic beers , sit at the table and not really talk to each other then leave , I thought ' surely not' but I kept a eye on them and sure enough they just sat there looking around , they got up to leave and as they left they decided to chat to me and Shane on the front door .. First of all it seemed normal then they started asking strange questions... like do we do drugs... and that we must do as it's well known that door staff do drug etc... Something wasn't right about this, it was also obvious that they was trying hard to talk like a commoner, I said "are you old bill or something, this is a strange convo", with that they laughed and walked off and we never saw them again.

A month or so later SIA (security industry authority), licensing and the police turned up to check on us, everything seemed fine. Tony went upstairs to get Jason, the police walked around the pub, checked our licences and went... all good...no problems, then Tony pulled me aside I could see from his face it wasn't good "mate Jason's dealing drugs"! , "what do you mean"? I replied, tony continued .. he told me he went upstairs to tell Jason that the SIA and the police was here and Tony saw the coffee table covered in drug bags and weight scales . I was in shock... more annoyed at myself that I didn't see it, but I was young and just starting out in the job, we all discussed what we was to do and we all argeed we couldn't afford to quit but we would start looking for a new job (what a horrible situation to be in), we certainly didn't want to lose our badges because of what we knew.

Something happened a few weeks later that decided for us.

It was Halloween night at the pub and we was busy, it seemed like a normal night till a few hours later when I was walking around doing checks .., I noticed there was a bit of a commotion at the front door, so I went over to see Shane and Paul refusing entry to a guy, then I noticed who the guy was.. A known drug dealer and he had previously glassed a doorman who worked here before us.

There was no way we was letting him in , it was twenty minutes arguing with the guy when the manager Jason came to the door and told us to let him in , I pulled Jason aside and no matter what I said he was adamant this guy was coming in, I spoke to Tony and he said " that's it I'm done " the other guys agreed to and we agreed we would walk from the door there and then, I told this to Jason and I think he thought we was bluffing but he agreed with us and the guy left or so we thought.

No Jason let him in through the back door, did he really think we wouldn't notice this scumbag.

I told the guys and we said "right! we are leaving", we shouted to Jason "bye we're off ", we got in our car and parked in the car park opposite the pub, watching Jason running around the pub kicking everyone out, it was quite amusing to see, I called the security company and explained everything and was shocked when he said "fuck them they can get another company to put up with that shit", he thanked me for all our hard work and that was that.

I then went on to work for a Canterbury based company called Falcon security owned by two guys called Mick and Steve, two really great guys , I really enjoyed working for that company , I'm not sure how long it ran for but it was a shame when they decided to close it down.

 I started by working a Friday and Saturday night at a place called studio 41, it was a interesting place to work and a really nice place to go clubbing with two rooms with different music.

The first room was more of a chill out area, and then you walked through a corridor past the cloakroom on the left heading to a big room with a dance floor and a seating area.

The guys I remember working with are... Darius (the legend), Darren, Simon, George and Carl.

Carl showed me around and said "the reason why they need a female door supervisor is to keep an eye on the female toilets and that's it", I'd gone from working at places restraining people to being told I was a toilet attendant , I was offended and felt like I was second class or something but this was a job and I needed the money.

I spent my time there either standing outside the toilets or at the top of the stairs collecting tickets for entry , after a while I got very bored of doing this then one night pushed me over the edge, I got a radio call from cctv (cameras) to go into the female toilets and remove a male that they had spotted going in there, so I went in and was very polite about it but the male kicked off with me saying " I'm the fucking DJ , me and my girl are fucking and I can do what I want so fuck off ", even the management agreed with him so I quit this venue, it didn't really surprise with the managements attitude towards this as on there gay night there they would have a room called ' the dark room ' , in there was soft porn on the tvs , big birthing balls where guys would go to have sex with each other (illegal of course) but somehow they never got caught.

I carried on working for falcon at different places , there was a house gas explosion in a close in Canterbury and falcon got the contract to look after the area till it was secured, great pay an hour, two guards twenty – four hours a day, one would sit in a shipping container converted into a mobile unit and the other would sit in one of the garages connecting to the houses to stop looting, when it was my turn to work in the garage I would take my German shepherd dog called shadow to work with me .

I would sometimes work with a woman called Rihanna, she was tall with long blonde hair and she was hard as nails.

 One night when I was off me and a work colleague thought we would have a laugh and went to the site in the dark, we started banging on the unit, Rihanna jumped out with a stun gun in her hand shouting "who the fuck is there?" it's lucky we didn't get tasered by her but it was funny at the time.

I did a few student venues and events for them but after awhile they decided to call it a day , it was such a shame , great owners and a great company to work for , still to this day I have my falcon polo top in my wardrobe .

I then got a job at a company called reboot , I started at weatherspoons in Canterbury working with a guy called Dean, a really nice guy and I learnt a lot from him he was laid back, calm and very good at his job, I was there for a couple of months then the guy I replaced came back and I moved on, I went to a bar called haha's with a guy called carl, a big friendly bear, I loved working with him, it was sad to hear a few years ago that he passed away .

I also worked in a few places in Ashford , then there started being problems with wages, I wouldn't be paid and they still expected me to get to work the wages paid my bills and to get to work, I didn't put up with it for long and found a job with gem security at a gay pub/club in stood, three to four shifts a week and at fourteen pound a hour which was a good wage not like todays which is less, it was a very friendly place and again filled with regulars, I fitted in well and being gay myself helped.

 Our main problem at this club was people having sex, for some reason because it was a gay bar they seemed to think it was fine to have sex there, it would happen in the toilets, garden, even sometimes the dance floor, it did used to gross me out, why would someone want to have sex in a toilet where people take a shit ?, maybe I'm just a prude.

I first caught two females in the toilets, I went in to check and saw some feet sticking out of the bottom of the door, the door had frosted glass and there was a very small frame around the glass that wasn't frosted and you could see in, so I looked and saw a female going down on another female, I banged on the door and said " security open the door please " , they got dressed and came out , I said to the younger one " what do you think you are doing ?" (Wish I never asked like that) the reply came "licking her out init", with that description and the state of the pair of them I neatly vomited in my mouth, they were both asked to leave for the night.

To stop the nightly occurrence of males having sex in the garden I would get a huge torch and walk around the garden using it, I caught a lot mid flow and it soon put them off. It was a lovely pub in the daytime, nice food, the garden had a seating area with a river view, only drawback was sometimes the place was prone to flooding due to being right next to the river, I remember it being on the news one year and they had to rip all the carpets up, did them a favour really.. Shouldn't have carpets in a pub that's also a club, the carpets end up really dirty and makes the place stink.

It was really enjoyable working there, some customers instead of buying us a drink they would buy what you call ' ready to drink receipts' that we could use anytime, so we would save them up and go on a night out there on our day off.

Even now at the age of twenty two nearly twenty three I was still a bit naive about things that happen, how drunk people get, rude and abusive, fights over nothing, I remember a girlfriend hit her boyfriend over the head with her heel shoes...blood everywhere.. Apparently she wasn't happy that he wanted one more drink before leaving.

Due to rising problems in town we was told we would be doing 100 per cent searches each night for a few weeks , I remember one of those nights when I asked a few for a search she flashed her police badge and asked if that made a differences I said no and carried on searching her , as much as I respect the police , there not all straight as the thin blue line , I used to get my fags and copy dvds of officers.

We nearly left someone in the club one night, a member of bar staff alerted us that a male was asleep in the toilets, the image is still burnt into my mind of a ginger guy sat on the toilet with his trousers round his ankles, you couldn't see his penis as his ginger pubic afro was so big, we went to wake him up and he wasn't at all embarrassed by it.

There was tension between our manager Diane (who would work the door with us) and the pub manager Phil, I liked Phil he was a typical gay queen, very hyper with amazing energy.

There would be times when they would argue, one night I can't remember why the place got dead so early but Phil said to Diane "as you guys are doing nothing and I'm the one paying you", you guys can sweep and mop the floors", of course Diane wasn't having that, eventually she lost the contract with them, I think it was mainly as she was charging nearly thirty pounds a hour for each doorman.

A company called Quality security took over the contract and contacted me saying that manager Phil had requested me and Tony to return there (which was really nice of him) , the pay went down to twelve pounds a hour but we got more shifts so it evened out well.

Now that I was on the front door as Diane wasn't there anymore, I realised the issue she had to face every night but again another chance to learn.

There was other pubs and clubs in the town about ten minutes walk from our venue, so people who got turned away in town or kicked out , their last option was for them to come to us , there would be a large group of rough looking straight males come to our door and we would turn them away, the assistant manager mick would spit feathers, he's a guy that doesn't want to hear what you have to say, he would say what he wanted and walk off before you had a chance to reply, so it was very hard with him.

We started to struggle in getting and keeping decent door staff, we had a guy called mike, he was a good friendly doorman, talked a load of crap sometimes but he was harmless. He only stayed with us for a few weeks then moved to a club in town.

Mike popped in one night when he finished early, it was nice of him to come and see us , he went and got a pint and chatted with some locals, later on a member of bar staff came over to me and said " Mike is doing coke in the toilet's", I thought surely not.. Would someone... a doorman in uniform at a place where he is known... being disrespectful doing that.., so I thought sod it I'm walking into the men's , there he was sniffing a line of coke off the sink.. I went fucking mad and told him to leave... the shocker... he really couldn't see what the problem was and was giving us all abuse as he was heading out the door, outside he started making threats against me (where the hell was this coming from) he kept coming towards me like he was about to attack, then from nowhere he took a swing at me.. I managed to duck but he kept trying, I then took a swing and hit him in the jaw, it finally stopped him, I felt bad... not for hitting him but I knew it was an unprofessional thing to do but it was self-defence. I phoned our boss Steve up and told him everything that happened and of course mike got sacked and we never saw him again.

Then Ricky came and joined us, he was a young lad, very nice and a good team player but he wasn't what he seemed, he lasted a month with us till we found out his SIA badge was fake then he was arrested and put in prison for stealing ambulance uniform and equipment, he was pretending to be a paramedic, he was caught when he tried to steal an ambulance vehicle.. How bizarre.

Amy then joined us , she was ok but not really a bouncer and I wasn't happy that there was three of us and two was female, its tough being a female bouncer but to have two on a team was silly but the company couldn't get anyone else to work there.

We was all working one cold night when a guy and two girls came to the door and I knew the male had previously been barred , the guy said his barring had been lifted and to get the manager which we did, I told Mick I wasn't happy for the guy to be in as he had previously beaten up another customer, but Mick had the final say as Phil was out and let the guy in, thirty minutes later Mick came to the door and asked us to remove the same guy (I thought great you idiot) , so Amy came and swapped with me and Tony and we went in , Amy could also see us from where she was stood at the front door. I thought I would talk to him first being female try to sort it out calmly rather then big Tony chatting to the guy, I explained that management wasn't happy and wanted him to leave for the night, the guy was very quiet and had his head down avoiding eye contact , I didn't expect what was going to happen next, he suddenly hand palmed me in the chest and I went flying back and fell on the floor , the guy took a swing at Tony and knocked him clean out and ran out of the side door, I quickly checked Tony was ok, he started to come round , I left him with the bar staff and went to find the guy, as I went out the side door I felt something wet fly across my face, I looked to the right and saw the guy was punching a random customer, more blood flew at my face and I froze for a second, the guy then suddenly ran off up the road, I went and helped the customer as an off duty copper phoned the police, I then went back to check on Tony who was sitting in the cellar, luckily he was fine, I later found out Amy had gone and hid in the toilets, due to this incident me and Tony was removed from the doors there but Amy got to stay , makes sense don't it ?.

Chapter 2

I took a month off the doors then went to work for a big security company in Canterbury where I knew I was going to learn a lot and was very excited about it, Tony didn't join with me he went on to do his own thing.

I started in am small pub in the town , a two man team , I only lasted a month or two there, the manager Gary took an instant dislike to me, I know its probably because I wasn't your typical dolly bird door woman.. I'm quite plain... I wouldn't say I'm ugly but nothing much to look at , so I think that was why, but I worked hard and was good at my job, so one night I turned up two minutes late..(Honestly by two minutes) I'm a person that is never normally late for work but this gave him an excuse to get rid of me, he came marching to the door and said "you're late I don't want you here, leave", what a asshole,, he did me a favour really as at that time I was only working two shifts a week at that pub so I got moved to a university night club and got four to six shifts so cheers Gary! (Knob)

I loved it at the university club, the university made sure the students was looked after, there was more of a customer service going on and I enjoyed helping people. The head door there was also one of the managers of the company was a guy called Nick who was mid thirties ex-forces and strict which made the place run smoothly.

There was fourteen to eighteen door staff depending what the night was event wise, there was three floors, top floor was a chill out room with sofas, pool table and a kitchen where people could get chips and burgers, what an awesome idea to have that inside a club, then the balcony which over looked the bottom floor where the dance floor was and don't forget this was the time where you could smoke inside clubs (saying this makes me feel old)

So I'm twenty four and slowly starting to enjoy this job, it was hard though because females still wasn't thought of as much and that we only really dealt with drunk females, so I really had to prove myself and also not being good looking made it harder , a lot of the time I was treated as useless and it made me feel like I was only there to make up the numbers , but I mostly expected it because I didn't have a penis swinging between my legs I wouldn't get accepted in this industry but at least I was making good money.

Every night there Nick would give us all a time list of where we was meant to be and when so there was no slip ups or mucking about, I learnt so much from him and what you should and shouldn't do, what is expected , how to be a decent doorman (door woman whatever!).

When Nick was head door it ran smoothly, I'm not saying the other head doors didn't do well but Nick ran it a military way and it worked out very well, and unlike the other head doors he didn't choose by who his friends were or brown nosing. Obviously with him being a manager he couldn't continue to be head door while working daytime in the office so after a couple of months it was passed onto a guy called Sean, he was a good doorman but towards the end he was a bit lazy and would sit in the back office chatting most of the shift .

 Over time door staff came and went, some wasn't suited for that kind of place by being too heavy handed and unprofessional, I remember a fight on the dance floor , we all ran in and two doorman Ron and Adam took two guys up and another guy was still trying to kick off so me and another female called Tanya restrained him and waited for back up as the dance floor was rammed, Ron came back and we gave the male to him and followed him out through the crowd, Ron was really losing his temper.. somehow they tripped in the crowd and I saw Ron wack the guys face on the floor, they then got up and continued upstairs, not long after I was called upstairs and was spoken to by Sean and manager Jean asking me what I saw, I know it was wrong but I said I saw nothing, I had only been with the company a few months would they be happy with me ratting on a guy that was seen as a top doorman, I know I would have lost my job so I kept my head down and out of trouble as much as I could, but I did regret it later on, we had a kick off outside and there was a radio call for all doorman to the front door.. I saw Ron run outside and ran up to a guy and just punched him in the stomach (what the?) I had a quiet word with Sean about that, and then Ron was sent into town... I couldn't turn a blind eye again, the guy he punched had nothing to do with the fight (not that it would have been justified if he was) but he was a innocent guy just standing there watching and getting punched by a doorman who is there to protect him is out of order.

 There was another time I had to speak up, we had a fight outside and the club was informed that a doorman was seen punching a load of students...i didn't see this but found out after as the doorman was bragging about it and had cuts on his knuckles from punching people, I was working after the club was shut when Jean asked me if I knew anything.. I really respected her and asked her to keep it between us, she told me members of bar staff had seen it, I told her I got to the incident after it happened but told her what I knew , there is a difference to apply a painful hold on someone but to physically hurt someone was not on.. I did the job to help and protect people we shouldn't be hurting people, anyway he got removed for that.

This night I got a call from Adam to meet him at the bottom of the stairs, a female had been asked to leave for being intoxicated but she refused to move, so I spoke to her and asked her to come with me but she kept refusing, so I told her "it's your choice you can come up on your own or we will have to assist you and bring you up ourselves", she finally agreed.. I didn't need to touch her but I put my hand behind her back in case she fell backwards as she was quite wobbly , she was taken to what we called an incident room, we was really busy so she was on her own in there for a few minutes (I wasn't allowed to go in as I had brought her up, its something that we used to do) when manager Jean went in the female asked her to call the police stating that I had assaulted her, the female had red marks and scratches on her left arm, what the girl didn't realise was the incident room had a CCTV camera, so Jean watched the footage of the female in the room and saw the female punching and digging her own nails into her arm (thank god for cameras ah!) these are the kind of lies that could ruin someone's life just because we ruined her night for her own safety, that's just one of the things we have to put up with in this job.

Another crazy night was a R and B night and it was rammed, halfway through the night a radio call came through " door staff to reception" " all door staff to reception", I arrived to see five door staff trying to put this massive guy to the floor , I kept moving people on etc.. While watching, then a doorman called Ross came running over and started punching the guy in the face quite a few times, I couldn't believe it and thanks to this there was consequences , the next night I was sat in the cctv room chatting to the cctv operator Rachel when for some reason we looked up at the front door camera to see about fifteen guys run at the front door, Rachel immediately called for all doorman to the front door, I rushed out and supported Chris and Tanya , we was like a rugby scrum trying to push them back out the door, other doormen arrived and helped , two male colleagues got pulled out by these men and got hurt by them then shockingly Rachel spotted something through cctv " 0guys careful one of them has a knife" thankfully it was a fake knife like a homemade Halloween one, this incident felt like it went on forever, Rachel had called the police but like always they left before the police turned up.

I didn't do too badly during that year but I wasn't given a chance to prove much of myself... I was either on the smoking area or top floor, I was only ever down stairs in the club area for a maximum of thirty minutes throughout the whole night.
Sometimes when head doorman Sean was off we had a replacement called Sam and he would put me on the smoking area for the whole five or six hours shift, one week with him in charge I spent twenty five hours that week just standing by the smoking door , I really hated that and it was embarrassing when customers asked why I was the only door staff that didn't to move about , it made me feel like shit, at least he was only in charge sometimes, Sean came back and we went back to normal for

awhile, for me it was now six years in total doing this job and was still enjoying it but I wanted a chance to prove myself .

Nicole then joined us she was twenty three years old, slim and looked like she could be a model, the guys was like flies round shit when she was about, and unlike me always stuck on a position for most of the night , she was straight away put on the clubs response team (that gutted me quite a bit) all about looks rather then if your good (not saying she wasn't but she didn't need to prove herself at all) but hey I needed the money so I stuck it out.. It was hard but eventually I was moved to the front door when Caz left, I've got to mention about Caz oh my god she was a right laugh, scary at times, She got stuck in and was never afraid, she was in her forties with short brown hair and smoked like a chimney much like me, we used to have such a laugh and her laugh would make you laugh that kind of thing.
 I remember when we was trying to get a female out of the toilets that had fallen asleep due to intoxication, manager Jean was standing behind us , this female was covered in sick with her pants and tight around her ankles .. I said to Caz "you sort the bottom and I'll do the top"... her reply "sod off, I'm not pulling her pants up", we was in hysterics, not at the poor girl but at the situation of our funny argument, sometimes all we had to do was look at each other and we would start laughing, it was a shame when she left I had learnt so much from her, I think she just had enough of it all.

So I was now on the front door , I finally felt like I was part of the team rather then a outsider now, I had my say, my voice and a chance to learn the front door of a very big nightclub and at that time I think the capacity was about 1500 and the place used to be rammed from Wednesday to Saturday.

 On Monday and Tuesday only top floor was open for live bands and they only needed three door staff but I was quite happy with my four shifts , it was quite stressful on the front door and very fast paced but I did enjoy it , checking ID's , refusing entry , answering questions, we didn't get much abuse back in those days not how it is today.

I was on the front door with a guy called Bruce , early twenties, very big and muscular, he was such a nice guy, he became like a brother and I felt safe with him , he did the seven o clock starts and was the one who stayed when we finished and he would only finish when the manger of the club finished which sometimes was as late as five in the morning .

Bruce was a great friend and helped me when a doorman started stalking me , so let me tell you what led to this.., I was on a event bus going home and one of the guys called Andy was with us he was changing his top in front of us and everyone was having a bit of banter, I commented on how good his six pack stomach looked (and that's how it started) he would then suddenly appear where I was working to see me, he would walk home with me even though he lived the opposite way , it was starting to freak me out, he nearly started a fight with Bruce because of how close I was with him, Bruce ended up having a chat with Andy about it and thankfully he ended up leaving me alone.

I paid Bruce back in a way by setting him up with a woman he went on to marry and have a family with, she's called Marisa and came to work with us, a really nice girl, they both spoke to me about how they like each other but was to shy to tell each other so one night I said " Bruce you're driving Marisa home" then told Marisa that Bruce was driving her home and the rest is history , over time they both left to start a new life in Croydon.

When Bruce left I got to take over his long shifts and also did the Monday and Tuesday shifts so I was on quite a lot of money each week.
 I've got to mention in this book about a doorman called Ashley, he was like a old school doorman and didn't believe a woman should be doing this job and even told me that , then one night cctv spotted Ashley needing assistances on the stairs, I ran past a useless doorman who was just standing there watching Ashley struggling with this guy, I got to Ashley on the stairs and saw despite him locking the guys arms up but the guy had hold of the bannister with one hand, so I got the guy's hand off locked that arm and helped Ashley take him up the stairs to the incident room , I went back to the front door , sometime later Ashley came over to me and shook my hand and said " sorry about what I said , I take it back " , bless him , after then we used to talk a lot and he was a real gentleman, telling me how he just wanted to meet someone and settle down and have kids, I really liked him, the sad thing is he ended up with a brain tumour I didn't know much about it but I didn't like to ask (others said it was due to him taking a lot of steroids) , after we heard this he came up to visit us at the club one night, club management wasn't happy about it.

I remember being shocked when I first saw him, I knew him as a muscly guy, but he was now really bloated and very bloated in the face, someone said the treatment that he was having does that to you. He stayed with us for the whole shift and you could tell he wanted to help us and get involved bless him, some of us spoke about him at the end of the night and someone said he had come to see us to say goodbye and a few months later he passed away.

I decided not to go to his funeral as its tradition for all door colleagues to stand together but I found out some people who used to always bad mouth him was going (why do people do that, hate on a person then go to their funeral) so I didn't want to stand with them so I didn't go but thought of him that day.

A couple of years past and I was one of the few remaining longest serving door staff at the club ,
 now they needed a new head door, was it me? no, they had choose a female that had only done door work for a few months , she was in her forties and they thought she would be a good fit as she had been a supervisor for a group of cleaners, I don't know how that works , not being funny but she had no experience in door work , so it was a bit strange, they annoying thing she got all my shifts, I still worked there, but I no longer opened up and closed so I lost quite a bit of money, they gave the hours to her , she was ok I guess but lack knowledge of the job, she came up with silly ideas that just didn't work, and she would allow drunk people in, we would have a set to when I turned this female away , she was very intoxicated and was staggering in her flat shoes , I turned around and jenny was stood there with the female saying to me " I think she's ok can we let her in " , I said no she's drunk, jenny replied " well I've done the nose test on her ", I still refused , after that the female gave me a lot of abuse, I'm not surprised as I was saying no and jenny was saying yes and this kept causing lots of problems , I asked her what she meant about ' the nose test', it was the test American cops would do when they believe a driver is drunk and would get them to lean back arms out stretched and touch there knows, what the fuck ! , I'sve never seen a doorman ever do that, it was obvious that girl was drunk and that was enough to know not to let her in.

As I said she meant well but she really shouldn't of been head door, she didn't last long there was quite a few complaints from the clubs manager, a few was to do with the locking up, on the fire doors you had to wrap chains around it, when I did it I made sure the chain went all the way round so there was no way anyone could open it, when jenny did it she would just hang the chain around so if someone opened the fire door from the outside they could easily just slide in, she then became student liaison officer and would hang around outside, that job didn't last long either, I don't know what happened to her after that, her son used to work on the doors with us, he was a good doorman, he was quite young, but he was bald and tall and a bit muscly, so we felt quite safe when he was on with us , I'm not even sure what happened to him he just seemed not to be there one day and that was it.

Was I bothered that I wasn't choose to be head door at the club, at that time not really I didn't think I was ready.

Over time I had random people on the door with me then a guy called Alfie joined us, he was in his fifties and was grossly over weight , he was put of the front door as he couldn't do much walking because of his knees, he took over my job and I was to assist him , he got his own way due to his mate now being head door a guy call Kevin.

Alfie was so lazy and he used to go for a cigarette break every twenty minutes, anyway we carried on regardless of his behaviour and I would just have to pick up his slack.

Alfie would rub other doormen up the wrong way , he acted like he was everyone's boss and was so rude to people , at the end of the night once the club was cleared all the doorman would put on high-visual coats and move the customers on outside and this night Alfie pushed another doorman too far a guy called Tom , at the end of the night he kept shouting at Tom telling him to hurry up and move people on , I stood there watching in disbelief as Tom and Alfie started pushing each other then Tom put his hands up in a boxing stance , thankfully the head door came out and pulled them apart , that was a first for me to see doormen fighting between themselves .

At this time I was also looking for some day work and Kevin asked if I would like to do some retail security in town, I was well up for that but

Nicole spoke to Tim our company owner and she got the job instead, she messed it up after a couple of months and got removed from there, sod it I didn't want it after that, I was on good money on the doors anyway I just fancied a change.

There was a period of months when I had to go on cctv for the club as there controller had left, I said I would do it if I got the same pay as I had been getting and they agreed. I really enjoyed it but I missed being able to attend incidents.

As well as controlling the cctv cameras I had to write down all the incidents we had which could take sometime on a busy night. One night we had to evacuate the whole club as someone had pressed a fire alarm, so almost 1500 people stood outside in the cold while waiting for the fire department to do there checks of the club, as this was a possible delibate act I was allowed to go in first to view the cctv footage to see who had pressed the alarm.

On the footage we found a male standing under a camera at the top of the stairs, he was there for sometime, he then whacks the camera out of focus and presses the fire alarm , and guess what..? the silly lad was still waiting outside the club to be let back in. he stood out like a sore thumb, he had a white t-shirt on with certain writing on his chest, bright green armbands, black ripped jeans and a trouser belt that looked like a piano keyboard, he was taken to the incident room when he walked back in the club, at first he denied it till we told him it was on camera. I later heard he got kicked out of university for that, if it was true I do feel sorry for him, for a moment of madness but it can put lives at risk, after that the fire department put up signs in the club saying anyone caught pressing the fire alarm unnecessary could face up to six months in prison and/or £5,000 fine.

I was later put back on the front door as they had hired someone for cctv.

Back again working with Alfie and he was the one in charge of checking ID's with the barring list and he kept letting banned people in, I know it wasn't my doing but I was part of the front door team, on this night Craig from the office was head door and he caught someone banned inside because of Alfie but Craig decided to shout at me in front of everyone, Alfie had the cheek to turn around to me and say "oh was he banned?, sorry I just can't be arsed tonight" (what a asshole), it kept happening so I decided I wanted to go back inside , I knew it would be more relaxed then before, I was feeling like a spare part on the front door and was sick of getting it in the neck for Alfie's mistakes.

The next night it was just a two man team and it was me and head doorman Kevin, he was already annoyed that I was picked to work that night rather then his mate Alfie and he told me that too.

 we started to chat, I got on with him okish but he can be a right bully to people, I said to him I would like to go back inside he asked why and I just lied and said I was bored and wanted to be more involved.. he knew something was wrong and kept asking and asking so I just told him I was tired of being shouted at for Alfie's mistakes (remember they are good friends) Kevin went mental and said "right you can be removed from here right now I'm phoning the office, you stupid fucking dyke" as he stormed into the back office, I could feel tears in my eyes, I had done fuck all wrong, the tears were more from anger, so I just walked off the door and phoned our mobile patrol driver to tell him what happened, it all went to the office. We were both spoken to and he denied it all and said I walked off the door for no reason, so for a week I had no door to go to.

Alfie left after a few months and went into retail security; I later heard he was fired for watching porn on a company computer while he was meant to be working (gross!)

I then got asked to go to another big club; Nicole was there but got removed after a few weeks for her behaviour (yet again)

But first I should talk about when I used to do one shift there a week, along with the original full- time female.
This club had big strong bouncers, they had a really good team there and the female called Debs she was awesome... she scared me a little at first, I used to be on the front door at the side of the building and she was on the main door at the front.

I had fond memories of when it snowed and we all had a bit of a snowball fight.

Debs left when she fell pregnant , again Nicole got offered the place before me, but as she got removed I went straight there from the last club, I would say its one of the best clubs in the south east, they knew how to throw a party and what people wanted.
You couldn't have asked for a better security team or management so again... everything happens for a reason.

The head doorman Marcus was a quiet guy, grade one hair, goatee, average height for a guy and a quiet ninja; he doesn't really lose his temper and is very quick at reacting to incidents, his second in charge Sam... late forties and such a amazing funny guy, strong and about six foot tall and the kind of guy that can always put you in a good mood with his wit and funny stories it wasn't always what he said , it was the way he said it, so entertaining, he told us a story about his daughter who had just past her driving test and she had got her first car during the winter time.

 he told us he had brought her a can of de-icer and after a few days she said to sam that she had run out and he couldn't understand how she had used it all in a few days, he later found out she had been spraying it all over the car and not just the windows.

 I got to work on the front door with them, it was quite daunting working with these amazing guys the first half of the night I would be doing searches then the rest on the front door with the guys.

Chapter 3

We had random kick offs there like you do in any club in the country.
 But first I want to go back a bit before telling you about the place.

 I also did some events and one I did was a county show at this one Prince Edward was attending, it was interesting to watch the royal security team check everything before he arrived, there was a embarrassing Mr Bean moment when I was running to a incident, I ran around the corner and I almost ran into him, I had to launch myself out of the way.

At the same event later in the day me and a guy called Robin was asked to ride around on bikes, so we could check on staff and get to incidents quickly, near the end of the day we assisted an elderly lady with finding her car as she had spent ages walking around the car park. She told us the make, colour and registration, we spent thirty minutes in the pissing down rain pedalling these bloody bikes around the muddy car park looking for this car and we couldn't find it then she remembered she brought her husbands car instead, me and Robin was like drowned rats thankfully we had now finished our shift.

I enjoyed some events, but most of our events was very long and hard, you would never get a break and the people chosen to be supervisors was very lazy and selfish and would get annoyed if they had to cover us for a toilet break .

At one event we had been working very long hours and was due something to eat, our company had been given food vouchers by the event company to give to us so we could get a burger and a drink, but how bad is this, our supervisor had given them to his family that came to the event so we had to go without food.

The worst event I ever did was a two day festival in Chigwell, I had to finish a door shift in the early hours of the morning then me and my other half Helen had to go straight there to this event and we was going to be camping there, it was meant to be a twelve hour shift starting at seven in the morning, but the first day ended up being a eighteen hour shift and we only had a twenty minute break , the only place to get something to eat was from a burger van which was a ten minute walk into the sleeping camp, so we got some chips and had to eat them as we walked back then I got told off for going to the toilet quickly, I was struggling on no sleep, little food and had been drinking lots of cans of redbull and took quite a few caffeine tablets, at about ten at night we had to go into a tent where a rock band was on and we had to go in and hold up the barriers at the front of the stage for the last song when everyone was moshing, I started to feel unwell , I managed to last till the end then I walked out of the tent and passed out . some first aiders came and got me in what I can only describe as a golf buggy and had to go back to the first aid tent , we was driving over bumps and holes and I thought we was going to tip over, I even kept putting my foot out ready for it to tip , we got back to the tent and I couldn't stop shaking , I told them that I probably over did it with the drinks and tablets and they agreed and said they think I should go home, I told them that the company wouldn't allow that, and they even spoke to the supervisor to tell them I needed to go home , but of course I wasn't allowed , I then met up with Helen and we went to our tent for the night but it took us awhile to get to sleep as a police van was parked right near us and kept making silly noises down there megaphone until a colleague of ours shouted out his tent " oi , shut the fuck up we are trying to sleep" the police van then slowly drove away.

The next morning I felt so rough, I was on the front gate with a older guy in his fifties who told me he had just gotten over swine flu, I thought great and I've got to work with him . I was so happy when the shift was over and we went home.

Two days later I was really ill and my temperature was high, yep you guessed it I had caught swine flu; I was off ill for the next week.

Not many problems happened at events really but I do remember one, at a beer festival, again we was lied to and told it was a twelve hour shift that turned into a eighteen hour one, late in the evening there was a gang of male youths that climbed the barrier and sneaked in, we had spotted them running, load of us attended , the thing that sticks out in my mind was a eighteen year old steward got punched and knocked out right next to me and he hit the ground with his eyes open , it scared the crap out of me but he was ok.

We also did a bike race in London, I had done a day shift previously somewhere I can't remember and I quickly went home to have a nap but our neighbour was being noisy as always, I tried to sleep, i think I only got about thirty minutes and had to be at the office for eleven at night, we left the office around midnight and got to the site around three in the morning and we was due to finish around seven or eight in the evening.

I was walking around like a zombie but luckily I got to walk around with Marcus (head doorman from the club) , we talked a load of rubbish throughout the day but it got us through it , think it was about eleven at night when we got home.

 I kind of gave up on events and only did them when I really needed the money , but if I was due on my period then I would turn down the shifts , not worth the hassle of worrying and not being able to go to the toilet , you just wasn't looked after at all, it was really tough at times ..I don't think I could do them now at the ages of thirty five I wouldn't be able to cope with no breaks , no food and hardly any water , the worse event for that was a big event we did up north , it was a four day shifts , it was very good money but didn't know just how bad it would be , we was told it was going to be 12 hour shifts but again it was a lie and ended up being 18 hours then a 2 hour ride home , so we got back at five in the morning and had to be at the office for 8, I hadn't eaten all day as we wasn't allowed to have a lunch break, so I quickly eat some junk food and got about a hours sleep , then back to the office . it was just as bad that day too, no breaks, if I had known it would have been like that I would of brought some protein bars .

Anyway the second day with no food breaks, we got toilet breaks and that was it.

I felt so drained that night. The next day at our briefing I brought up about not having no food breaks, the owner of the security company was shocked and apologised and said it would be sorted and that we would be having breaks that day, later on me and a guy called Paul was on the main gate searching, we was basically stopping people from bringing in any alcohol, it got to half way through our 18 hour shift when the supervisor told me to get into the van, so I did and asked where we was going, to which he replied " nowhere your are to have your 20 minute break in here, so I said " oh I'm just going to get my food from our security hut" which was about a 2 minute walk from where we was, he said that I wasn't allowed , I couldn't understand it, we wasn't allowed to have our bags on our positions so left them in the hut, I said sod my break then and went back to the gate , Paul went to the van for his break but came back within in minute with the van driving off, Paul was livid " what the fuck is this shit , sit in the van but not allowed to get our food , they treat us worse than slaves".
We was both starting to feel rough from lack of food, I came up with a idea , I said to Paul, " if we are carefully we will stop the next lot coming in with food ", thankfully the next few people had some sandwiches, I felt bad but neither of us had eaten in two days, so we managed to have some food. I pulled out of the final shift I couldn't cope with it , it worked out well as I swapped with someone who was working locally and was less hours, I would never do that event again, I think what the problem was, was that the supervisors was meant to cover us for our breaks but they didn't want to and didn't bother.

I heard at an air show which was a very hot day, that 5 officers fainted as they had no shelter from the sun and wasn't given water, that was the kind of thing we was expected to put up with, but if you need the money you would do it.

So back to the big club, it was a great place to learn and grow, I always got stuck in, but I was mainly protecting the guys during fights, like when customers tried to attack them while they was restraining people, we worked as a good solid unit and we could rely on each other, I felt very safe there.

I have a few fond memories like when a guy got kicked out for his behaviour and outside he was going mental and a police officer was there looking panicked, so me and Sam went over to assist him with the guy, the officer got his cs spray out and went to spray the guy but it sprayed sideways and went over me and Sam, luckily it wasn't too much.

We had a guy that had been in a fight and was kicked out but he kept trying to come back it was a funny moment like a game of rugby, the guy ran past Sam who tried to grab him, then past me .. No luck... then he was about to run past Marcus when Marcus puts out his hand and smacks the guy around the face, (not in a really bad why more like a tap to the side of the face) which stund him and stopped him in his tracks (remember he was still trying to get to this male to attack him) but I did find it amusing.

A bit of a moment was when one night we had the police licensing in the building having a look around, I went to the toilet and had just finished weeing when there was a call on the radio "all door staff to the front door immediately "... I ran out doing my trousers up as I went, there was a fight with three massive guys, Tim had one in reception, Marcus had one on the floor outside, I went over to assist Sam with another male who was really throwing himself about, I noticed there was a guy curled up on the floor in the corner of the smoking area, I found out what happened after we managed to get these guys sorted with the police that turned up.
so what happened was these guys were arguing with some other customers , Sam was chatting to them and calming them down but the two licensing police officers bounded over all cocky like flashing there badges and one of the big guys head butted the officer .. The other officer

ran inside the club, that's right the guy curled up on the floor like a baby was the other officer.

The grossest incident at this club that I had to deal with was when I got a call from cctv for me and my colleague Holly to go to the female toilets as the controller had spotted on cctv a female dressed in a bin bag (students will dress up in anything) who was very intoxicated going into the toilets, myself and Holly went into the toilets and the smell hit us straight away, Holly was gagging and couldn't deal with it and went outside and waited, a customer pointed to a toilet cubical where the door was ajar , I pushed it slowly open to see a female squatting down facing the toilet being sick and under her ass was a massive pile of runny poo (shaped like a cowpat) I told her who I was and she needed to sort herself out and come out of the toilets , imagine the smell of baby poo that's what the smell was like. I gave her a few minutes then reopened the door, there was a poo ring on the floor where the cowpat was, she must of scooped it up in her hands and put it down the toilet, she staggered out and I noticed she had little bits of poo all over the bin bag she was wearing, the stench was unreal.

There was a massive queue to use the sinks and she asked if she could wash her hands... I couldn't handle the smell anymore my eyes was watering, so I was a bitch and said no and escorted her out of the building, I did managed to find one of her friends who was equally disgusted .

Most bizarre incident was when two men who had been fighting by the bar, two straight men (you'll understand why I put that in a minute) one managed to bite part of the other males tongue off, one of the door staff had to go and look for it, he found it and put it in a bag of ice and gave it to the paramedics, the guy now talks with a lisp.

Another time we got a call to a female who had hurt her foot, this was back in the day when drink was still being served in glass bottles and glasses , we had to carry her down the fire escape which was a lot easier and safer for her with all the customers about, as we took her down the stairs, I was guiding the way making sure her foot didn't hit anything, I looked at the foot and I could see a massive chunk of skin and muscle was missing from her big toe and I could see her toe tendent , I made sure I blocked her view from seeing it as it freaked me out imagine how she would of felt seeing that,

she was taken away in a ambulance , unfortunately we don't always get to find out what happened to them , I really don't understand why she was wearing sandals to a night club , bound to get hurt somehow .

New years eve night came and like everywhere in town we was rammed , I got a call to deal with a female who said she had hurt her ankle , when I got there John another doorman came over to me and said " I just went to check on her and her reply was 'fuck off I'm fine' so I wouldn't bother ", but of course I did check on her , I shone a torch on her and said " I know you told my colleague your're fine but do you mind me checking"? and she agreed ,

 I ran the torch over her ankle and saw no marks or swelling so nothing I could see (but I'm not a doctor) I asked if she could move everything without any pain to which she said she could and told me it only hurt when she twisted it and that the pain was going, I got her some ice to put on it to help and told her to call me if she had anymore problems, she didn't seem intoxicated but was wearing like ten inch heel shoes that everyone wears . I went to check where she fell over to make sure there wasn't a spillage and there wasn't.

I knew there probably wasn't as the club was always on top with that but it was still good to check.

About forty minutes later I got a call about the same female that had fallen over again and this time her leg was hurting , so I went back to her and she was sat on a stool crying , I took a look at her leg and it was now very swollen and I knew something was wrong, I called for assistance and John decided to carry her down the stair as it was so packed that night, as John carried her down the stairs I could clearly see she had a broken leg as the broken bone was protruding out , a really dippy doorman called Ricky came running up the stairs and before finding out what had happened he grabbed hold and yanked the broken leg (for fuck sake) the poor girl screamed and passed out, we got her out the front and laid her down on some coats ,

 not long after a ambulance turned up for her, the poor girl was in so much pain, she asked me to ring her mum , which I did, her mum answered and I explained what had happened and that her daughter wanted her with her , the mother didn't really seem to care and just replied " fuck sake , well I can't drive I've been drinking " she was quite abrupt about it , I thought fucking hell this is your daughter and she's in a lot of pain get a fucking taxi, but she was acting like it was spoiling her night , I just ended the call telling her she would be taken to ashford A and E, the girl had apparently broken her leg in three places and tried to blame the club , which was a joke , ' how about you trying to walk in very high heels that you can't walk in and drinking think that's to blame really', we have all seen them kind of girls out for the night walking in heels like bamby and they expect to be able to get drunk and dance when they can't even walk in them and they try and blame others.

We had another one like that where she missed a step walking down the stairs and twisted her ankle , again only herself to blame with very high heels on , I got her to sit down and got her some ice to put on her ankle , I told her maybe she should call it a night and she was like " na the pain is going " she got up to show me and didn't limp and even did a little dance to make a point , again she wasn't what I would say drunk just merry she then went back inside the club.

 thirty minutes later she was hobbling out and got in a taxi with her friends, I later heard she broke her ankle and again tried blaming the club . I really hate those ' no win no fee' companies , people will try anything to get a bit of money out of someone but its wrong, if I fell over and it was my fault then I fell over it happens , end of .

I learnt a lot at this club , we had older customers as well as students.

One night it was the first night of freshers week (which is the first week for new students joining university) and it was like any other normal night so it was about an hour before last entry and I was standing in the foyer, when I heard a doorman called john radio, " call an ambulance, call them right now ", someone asked where he was , he replied he was on the stairs, I immediately thought as I rushed to the stairs that someone had fallen down the stairs and was seriously injured, I got there to see john helping a male down the stairs clutching his stomach, john said he had been stabbed, john rushed him outside to over the other side of the road, I radioed for some towels and then checked his stomach, there was a hole about three inches wide and part of his intestines was bulging through, there was hardly any blood and I think it was due to his intestines blocking the hole.

I asked him what had happened , he hinted that he knew who had done it , that it was a gang war from London but he refused to tell us anything else, he was taken away in an ambulance .

I headed back to the door and was asked to help a police officer and a colleague to keep everyone inside the club as the police wanted to video recorded everyone leaving for evidence, so there was me, an officer and another female colleague and we was holding the inner entrance swing doors closed with many customers on the other side pushing on it, I then had a stupid bright idea to wedge my foot against the bottom of the door, I got my foot stuck, thankfully it was a zip work boot and the police officer helped me pull my foot out, that could of ended really badly for me , we couldn't physically hold the door anymore and the customers spilled out onto the street.

I later heard the stabbed male was fine, and that there was a press release of a picture of two males they wanted to talk to about the stabbing but I don't think anyone was brought to justice for it.

It impacted on the club, the council put signs up on the club doors that the club's licence was to be reviewed, which I understand from a safety point of view but it wasn't our fault , we did searches and banned people who were trouble.

The day after the incident the club had 100 per cent searching in place, we was also to use wands, I was knackered every shift, we had to bend down and wand the whole person not just the upper body as well as searching through there items and we had to do it all at a quick pace as there was only two of us searching 1400 people, I had a lazy guy on searching with me , I can't remember his name so let's call him bob, bob thought he was too good to be searching and kept saying so " I should be inside I'm better than this " , I never understood why people think they are too good to search, I know it's not as exciting as breaking up fights, but it's a very important job, in the past I have found while searching people, knifes, knuckle dusters, drugs and alcohol that people try and sneak in , but if someone wants to get something in they will, there is only so much we can do , some stick it down there pants to get it into a club and obviously we can't search there.

A few days later we got a call that there was an issue on the middle floor, some of the guys went and after a while they brought out a guy that was being restrained and two people who's eyes were streaming, the guy restrained had snuck in pepper spray and had sprayed it about in the club, when asked why he had no reply, the police was called because 1, two people had been assaulted with this spray and 2, pepper spray in the uk is classed as a fire arm, the police was called but shockingly they didn't want to know, this was a club where I found the police to be very rude and unhelpful, I remember a time when the police was struggling with a few people they were arresting, I was asked to help a male officer restrain a female, so I did and held one of the females arms, when a female officer arrived she came over and said nothing and with her body she barraged me out of the way, I know there is always rude asshole in every industry but it seemed to become more and more common with the police , there was a guy whom the door staff caught sniffing coke in the toilets , he was asked to leave but refused and kicked off , then his friends kicked off , there was more of them then us so the police was called on the city radio, the police arrived and I was asked to relay what had happened, so I explained everything to the sergeant and I could see from the look on his face that he wasn't interested and he said " well I would kick off too if I was accused of doing drugs", what a great attitude for a sergeant to have, so despite the guy doing drugs and him and his friends assaulting door staff the police let them go , what's annoying the most is they would always disbelieve us if we had a problem with someone, but was quick to investigate if a punter falsely accused us of something, a few times someone would call the police and accuse me of assaulting them and the police would be there within minutes to investigate , again I was thankful for cctv to prove what's really happened.

Anyway so thankfully everything went ok with the clubs licencing review and we continued on as normal, except for we continued with the 100 per cent searches and had got a few more door staff.

It was at this club when I went through my most stressful time in my personal life, and one of the club's managers/owner was a great friend to me through this time, She really helped me get through it, I was ill at times, I won't go into what happened (maybe save it for another book) but I was diagnosed with acute PTSD and had inflammation all over my body but after a year I recovered well through counselling and therapy.

My shifts were cut back at this club, I don't blame them for it they were trying to save money, I think that the student fees going up and other pubs now had late licences effected how busy it was, so being female I was the first to get sent home and lose shifts, so I spoke to the security company and asked to go back to the student club.

My first night back at the student club the door staff had changed a lot , I really didn't know many people there, Tanya was there and it was nice to see her, I went in and went downstairs and within ten minutes the head doorman Dave called me to the front door, he told me as I was already trained on the front door and that the club management wanted to switch things about, they decided to replace Tanya with me for the front door, I did feel bad for Tanya as she had been there a long while and for them to suddenly replace her, I know what that feels like .

So I was now on the front door and I wasn't planned for this and I didn't bring a coat so I was a bit cold but I enjoyed it , The club started cutting back on staff so we had to rearrange the team and it left me on the front door on my own , managing the two queues which was quite stressful but I love stressful situations, Tanya was a great help as she became head steward and if I had refused someone entry and get them out of the queue I would give them to her and she would deal with it and I could get on with dealing with the queue, last entry would be at 12.30, so as soon as I got the two queues In I would then have a cigarette , I did love it, but missed being involved with incidents inside, after a while our head door Dave quit and was replaced with a guy called Steven, an awesome guy, ex-army, very good at the job, and he could run as fast as Usain bolt.. There was a time when a guy outside punched someone and ran off, Steven ran after him... I thought he won't catch the guy but a couple of minutes later he came around the corner with the guy.

Steven was a hard guy but sometimes he was a typical guy that needed a woman's help. I saw him walk into the incident room then he called for me to come in , he had a big cut above his eye brow, he had been walking through the dance floor and some female who was wearing a lot of rings was swinging her arms about dancing and accidently hit Steven, it was quite a deep cut, he asked me to just clean it for him, I said " you can't walk around the club with that cut on show, the cctv operator Rachel was trying to say to put a sanitary towel over it, Steven was like " fuck off I ant wearing that", I managed to sort it out and cut a bit off an eye patch with some bandaged and used micro tape to tape his cut shut , I did say he really needed to get it glued but he was too hard for that shit and he just let it heal naturally

It had been a few months since I left the last club and there was a guy I used to work with their called Chris, He was such a lovely down to earth guy, I could listen to him for hours, he was so spiritual, I was told the sad news that he had a fit and passed away, he was only in his thirties, I will always remember him

There was a few incidents there that stick out in my mind, me, Helen and Nicole went to the female toilets after getting a call that a female was passed out in a cubical, we found her and she was out for the count and had been sick, now normally I can put up with all different smells of sick (apart from shit smells) but this one was one of the worse, I checked her bag for her ID and found a hip flask , I opened it and smelt it, it was rum, no wonder her sick stunk , so we had to get her out but it was unsafe to take her up the stairs so we decided to go to the lift, we said to Nicole " you go with her and we will meet you upstairs", me and Helen ran upstairs to the lift, it pinged open and we was greeted with something out of the exorcist, the female was now slumped up against the wall and Nicole was standing in a star shape surrounded by sick everywhere all up the walls, floor and ceiling, Nicole was shouting "get me out, get me out ", it was comical .

Another night I was standing facing the dance floor near the end of the night waiting for the last song to finish playing, as the song slowed down to finish and the crowd parted I spotted a female at the back against the stage with her head tilted backwards, I was trying to work out what was going on, there was a guy standing in front of her, the music stopped and the lights went on and I saw it all, The guy had his hand down the girls trousers moving at a fast rate, the afro bush in full view.. I called my colleague John to come and assist, I approached them and told them to stop, John escorted the guy away, I looked at them and radioed John "careful John he's got blood on his hand", that incident traumatised me for weeks.

February the following year the security company lost the contract to the club I was working at and a new company took over, thankfully I applied to them and I joined them a week later, the last company I worked for was for eight years so this was a bit daunting going to a new team, I was back at the club but instead of the front door I went down stairs on to rotation, I knew one guy called Joe who I had worked with before which was nice, and it was nice that we rotated every thirty minutes which didn't happen with the last company I worked for, it stopped you from getting bored and kept you fresh and it certainly made time go quicker, there was fag breaks and the supervisor would bring you cups of water which was really nice and I wasn't treated any differently from my male colleagues.

This was the first time I used a body camera, I wasn't keen at first, not because of anything I do or say but just the thought of recording my common sounding voice, but I got used to it and thought they was great especially when someone would lie about something and the proof was on the body cam (it's like saying up yours without saying it) it protected us and protected the public, I liked it so much that I wish i could have one in my day job too, sometimes people would comply more when they notice they have a camera recording them, plus it was great evidence for the police and court, the one mishap I did have with a body cam was when I went to the toilet for a wee and when I finished I washed my hands and looked up at the mirror and noticed the body cam was recording, oh my god I had recorded me peeing, probably close ups of my knickers and everything, I tried to go on the viewing part of the camera to try and delete it but you can't, how embarrassing, I told the office about it which they found quite amusing but I didn't hear if they saw the clip, least my knickers was clean, I guess that was a plus, I always made sure i checked it wasn't recording before I went to the toilet in the future .

We had a few incidents that I remember , I was on the stage when I spotted a guy with a girl leaning against the speaker on the dance floor , she looked wasted and he didn't , she kept dropping down due to her intoxication and he kept propping her up against the speaker and kissing her, I was concerned about this and radioed my supervisor called Jim, he came over and I explained what I saw and that I was concerned for this female due to her level of intoxication and the males behaviour.

So myself and Jim went over to them and I tried to talk to the female and I do believe she was that drunk that she couldn't work out who I was and that I was just trying to look after her, she kept pushing me away and stumbling backwards, Jim got the male away but he was protesting as he wanted to be with the female, I managed to get her to move with me but she kept trying to grab Jim, we got to the stairs and I was trying to explain to her that she hasn't done anything wrong and we was just concerned and wanted to speak to them somewhere quiet, so we was all walking up the stairs nicely, then when we was a few steps from the top the guy just launched himself at Jim , then the female kicked off, she was actually trying to throw herself down the stairs,

She put all her weight and her foot on the ledge of the step and was trying to push herself backwards down the stairs, I had to hold on tightly to the bannister with one hand and with the other gripping on her arm to stop her from falling down the stairs, I thought fuck we could all end up falling or she's going to fall but there was no reasoning with her, Jim managed to restrain the guy and carry on taking him up the stairs, I managed to swing the girl up the stairs and managed to rebalance ourselves but as we got around the corner she started punching me in the face, I put her up against a wall, restrained her and took her to the incident room .

Chapter 4

Right! Number one I was fucking fuming that the cctv operator did not spot this, the last companies operator was shit hot on this and always spotted and watched us taking people out and called for assistance if we needed it, this was one of the reasons why we would radio that we was bringing someone out so cctv could watch us, number two, we was concerned for her wellbeing as she was very intoxicated and the guy was all over her and the situation ended like this and you know what that female put in a complaint that I had hurt her arm, if I hadn't of held onto her tightly she would of gone flying down the stairs due to her own fault it could have been a lot worse , the cheek of her.

I absolutely hated the stairs and there is always loads in most night clubs I've worked at, such a pain and so dangerous and my one fear is falling down them, so far I've been lucky and only fallen a few steps once at another club when a female refused to leave, me and a colleague had to restrain her and lead her down the stairs and she deliberately dropped her legs and I fell and the edge of the stairs hit me in the back, I had a massive bruise across my lower back that lasted for weeks.

It was great working with my supervisor, he was younger than me but had got the job down to a tee, muscly and he was right laugh, only downside was his farting, proper protein farts, he would come to your position, fart then walk off laughing, one time I told him he needed to check himself as it smelt like he shit himself, he ended up moving into town, he didn't do anything wrong, they just needed a strong male to join another team.

The club closed for summer and I got moved into town, I was happy and I got more shifts, this place was different and the managers didn't like me, I worked very well so again I think it was down to my looks, they used to talk to the other door staff but used to ignore me (fuck'em) , it was a nice club and another place to learn from with different clientele.

I was first put on the door where females normally get put but I think the manager said he didn't want me on the front door so I went inside on rotation.

One night when I was on the front door it was a doctors and nurses night out from the local hospital, everything was going well till one of the doctors was escorted out of the place, apparently he had assaulted someone another night and got banned, he went mental , he told us he was a surgeon at our local hospital and that if we ever went into his operating room he would make sure he got shaky hands, how sick is that, he was racist to all of us (we was all white british) he kept going on and on then he was arrested by the police. The police came back later on and told us he wouldn't be charged for being racist as you can't be racist to white people apparently.

This was where I noticed how important bodycams were, I had a call to the front door where a female was throwing herself about trying to assault door staff she was restrained and myself and another doorman held her until the police arrived, they was very off with us like we was in the wrong , until they saw the cctv footage of her behaviour then there attitude changed and the female was arrested.

I was there for about six months but had to move to the strip club as yet again Nicole got removed from their due to her behaviour, I was pissed , I went from five shifts to three, two at the strip club and one back up the student club.

I spoke to my boss about this and he said he was doing Liam a favour (as Nicole was dating him) and he was sort of part of management with the company/trainer... so me and Nicole swapped places, she popped up to see us one night and she told me she demanded more shifts and that's why we swapped places.. why did she even have to bring it up let alone lie about it, pissed me off even more to lie as I knew the truth as even the head door had complained and wanted her moved, so anyway back to three shifts, I did say I didn't want to stay at the strip club too long and if they found someone else that would be great and I would be happy going back to the student club, which management agreed with.

The strip club could have been a great place it was just so poorly managed, the first manager there that I worked with would sit upstairs the whole night gambling on a phone app, leaving the team leader Linda managing it, unfortunately I can't really talk much about what happened here, as there is a few bad things that happened but the place and owners are easy to identify if I mention them.

I was a bit shocked my first night, there was women walking around in their underwear, I didn't know where to look, I knew one of them and she was a nice girl, most of them was nice, a few totally crazy.

After a while I got quite protective of the girls, it was my job to watch the guys when they went in for their private dances, it was strange at first then I got used to it, some girls was classy others were really rough, I stayed there for a few months then they found another female that was happy to work there but I got used to it so it was a bit sad to leave.

So I went back to the student club, it had changed a bit since Jim left, A young guy called Craig had taken over as the supervisor he was just eighteen, he was a good doorman considering his age but he was a lazy supervisor, when his mates would work at the club he would forget to rotate us and he would be standing in the corner of the club chatting with them, I had spent a whole shift in the smoking area on a cold night shaking like a shitting dog, another night just guarding the toilets as it was out of order, we was never checked on , nothing.

Before I go on I need to tell you about the head doorman, called Karl, a lovely guy with a heart of gold , and very intelligent , but would always micro manage and never trust anyone to do the job themselves but then at other times he wouldn't check on the staff and things would get missed, we had quite a few run ins, once was with the bodycam , we was told every incident must be recorded, two guys was taking someone out and I turned on the bodycam and followed to record it, along the way Karl stopped me and told me to record the incident.. I was and now I had lost the guys and the incident wasn't recorded because Karl had stopped me.

If you knew what you was doing he would have to give you a play by play on everything , to the point that it was coming across as insulting , I don't think he meant to be like that though , I think it was just the way he is.

I spoke to the Karl about Craig a few times, he said he would have a word but nothing changed, same as like when I wanted to go to the toilet, I would radio for Craig to come to my location and sometimes I would be waiting over an hour, I had enough of it and asked one of the bosses of the company called Nick if I could move to another place , he asked if there was a problem where I was working and I explained in a nice way the reasons why and he called me and he was shocked and didn't know Craig was a supervisor and said someone with my experience should be, I replied I didn't really care who was as long as I could move around and go to the toilet when needed , I wasn't bothered about being in charge ,but Nick was adamant that I would be and said he would sort it out for the following shift.

So next shift the head doorman Karl came to me and said Nick had spoken to him but he wasn't going to change anything because it would be a kick in the teeth for Craig. I couldn't understand this, I said he hasn't been doing his job for a long time and surely if he's been spoken to then he has had his chances but Karl was adamant and it stayed the same until Nick came up one night and asked me why I wasn't running things downstairs and I explained what had happened, it changed the following week and I began to run it.

I really enjoyed finally moving around and dealing with things, Craig did take it on the chin and I tried to help him improve and put him as my second in charge and he did improve dramatically, things worked really well for a while then Craig started going out with a female door woman that was on the front door and his mind started to wander on the job or he would disappear and I would find him on the front door, I tried to be subtle to begin with, but it still kept happening, I had to have a second to cover me if I was dealing with an incident, I should be able to rely on them to sort out rotation, deal with problems and check on certain things, but I would come out of the incident room and see him chatting on the front door, I would then go down stairs to find no one has been rotated for an hour.

so my first time being a supervisor at the freshers week ball , I know I wasn't first pick as they already had names down on who was covering each area and there had already been a meeting between them all about it , I was asked at last minute , I was kind of chuffed but knew I wasn't really chosen they just didn't have anyone left that they could choose so I was last option.

Anyway I was put on the main tent which would have acts then later a silent disco, I didn't have a great team , but we didn't do too bad, had a few staff from another company but they was lazy and useless they might have been good in a fight , but we had so much more to do and that , and that was to use clickers so we could keep a eye on how many people was in the tent but I caught them many times too busy chatting to girls when people were walking in and out without clicking (I mean wtf its only part of our licence or could cause problems with over crowding) but they probably thought they was too good to click in and out, idiots.

inside the club had a act on and we was to have the next big act after and my concern was hundreds of people coming out of the club and coming straight over to us , I didn't want a stamped or for people to get injured , so I got staff to get some barriers so we could sort out a line and briefed some of the staff that was to be making breaks in the queue so we didn't get a crush , of course I swap those useless guys and just put them by the bar and toilets .

It's so lucky we did that because my prediction came true , we needed more staff so I radioed the head door to send some over and thankfully we controlled it , everyone knew what they was doing and everyone worked brilliantly.

 we was full when the act was on which was around 30 minutes , then most left to go back to the club for more music as now we was going to a silent disco with head phones, which we only had a couple of hundred in for that.

I enjoyed doing that , it was a new experience for me and I know I did well and everything went well.
I hoped this showed management that I was capable of doing things like this and next time I won't just be an after thought.

After I left that company and they had the same event they put someone in charge of the tent I did that had little experience don't get me wrong it's not their fault that things went massively wrong they probably tried their best , Bex who was part of management again with no experience of these events was trying to help with the tent but it went massively wrong, so this is just hear say from a good friend but its most likely what had happened.

So as before people came out of the club and over to the tent, they didn't have anything to stop people just rushing in the tent, apparently they had to link arms to try and hold everyone back, Bex went and got a metal barrier and was hitting it against people and had hurt a doorman by getting him trapped with it , apparently she had a break down in the end and ended up crying . shocking really but that's what happens with lack of experience and picking ass lickers instead.
Yes I had a bit of delight when I hear about town how badly they are performing but they really only have themselves to blame for treating the good staff the way they did and making them leave the company and are left with a few good ones but chose people that are not good at the job just because there friends, what's the saying?? There is no friends in good business, I'm sure that's not totally true but I'm sure it applies here.

You are probably thinking why is she being so horrible about her old team, well you will find out later in this book about how I was treated and you will see why, I'm honestly not a horrible person, well only if someone has pissed me off.

After the holidays we went back to the club and it was the same with Craig , we now had a new head door called Sarah (who is a legend), I decided to have a chat with Craig and knew he was good friends with Sarah and thought this would help when talking to him, I said to him " I really need your help in supporting Sarah , she's going to be a great head door and I don't want us letting her down", that seemed to work, he was smashing it.. an amazing doorman for his age, but again his girlfriend was influencing him and now for some reason his girlfriend Rachel and the other male doorman Phil who was on the front door with Rachel was bullying Sarah, Sarah told me the whole issue which was just paranoia and jealousy on Rachel's part and was being quite nasty to Sarah, I saw it for myself when I had to go to the front door to speak to Sarah about things inside, I saw them both in the corner whispering and laughing while looking at Sarah and leaving her out of conversations and just basically ignoring her, it was disgusting to see .

Sarah was already going through a hard time in her personal life and to get bullied at work is disgusting, I tried to help as much as I could, even know she was younger than me, I looked up to her and respected her and she didn't deserve the way they were treating her.

It went on for a while as I think the reason why is Craig is one of the bosses brother in law, but eventually Rachel got moved into town and my partner Helen got moved onto the front door, the bullying was still happening but from afar, things were made up that was meant to be happening at the club and myself and Sarah was getting stick about it.

One night we went for a cigarette and was talking about a few things including this and about situations inside the club as there was a few issues that needed to be sorted, all of a sudden one of our bosses that is Craig's brother in law called Aaron suddenly appeared out of the bushes and started shouting at us, I saw tears well up in Sarah's eyes and she stood up for herself and walked off, I was left with Aaron and i was trying to explain but he wasn't having it and had a right go at me, If it wasn't for Sarah and Helen working there I would of walked off that night, after all the people taking the piss, giving the company a bad name and he had a go at the two people that was keeping the place going, but unfortunately he trusted his brother in law with what he was saying, we never really found out what was said .

Craig continued to work with us but it was very strained he even refused to speak to Sarah and she was his boss so that was a joke, he couldn't seem to concentrate on the job anymore, I think his girlfriend put a lot of pressure on him.

I decided to start training another guy up to take over Craig if things got worse or he ended up leaving, I choose Simon, he was around Craig's age but he had a lot of discipline, I was impressed, so I spent a lot of time with him and slowly changed him and Craig, Craig did take it hard but he had so many chances and how could we expect the rest of the team to work hard when Craig wasn't and was just doing what he wanted, after a while Craig quit, I was sorry to see him go, he was a nice lad but was just young and got with the wrong girl (well a crazy girl to be honest) and made wrong choices, but thankfully after that things started running smoothly and Sarah was really starting to enjoy her job which was really nice to see, she's a great head door and she can see who is good at their job and trusted them to get the job done, more of a leader then a boss.

The atmosphere at the club between the staff was now really good, we had tough nights and other nights we would have a right laugh.

 One night we got a call to go to the female toilets, Me and Sarah went to find a female passed out in the toilet cubical, knickers round her ankles there was some poo all over her, we managed to sort her out and get her out the cubical, we put her in the recovery position while we decided how to get her out as it would need more than two of us (she was a big girl) all of a sudden we heard over the radio "evacuate" "evacuate", we looked at each other and said "shit", with all our strength we each took her arms and legs and tried to quickly move but this girl was all ass which was dragging on the floor , we managed to get out the nearest fire door and placed her down on the floor, then I realised we had put her down long ways, "Sarah people are going to be coming out this way, we need to move her", so we moved her our the way, then out boss Aaron came running down the steps to us " don't worry I'll move her ", acting like he was the milk tray man from the advert, Sarah shouted out " no Aaron poo!", but it was too late and he got it smeared on his shirt, that amused us loads, poor Aaron.

These sorts of incidents were becoming a regular occurrence, Females getting so wasted and ending up in a state trying to drink like men.

Another night I did a toilet check and heard a female being sick , I knocked on the door and identified myself and asked her to open the door, she was sitting on the toilet , I told her to finish and sort herself out then come out, I was waiting what felt like ages, I opened the door and she was still sitting there, I told her to hurry up and that she needed to get off the toilet, with that she got some tissue and wiped her ass and showed me the tissue while saying " I is shitting", I was so disgusted and told her that was disgusting thing to do and told her to hurry up, another five minutes passed, I opened the door again to find her playing a game on her phone....i wasn't having that, so I took the phone off her and told her to come out, with that she sorted herself and finally came out, I still can't believe she did that, disgusting girl.

Another disgusting sight was when we had a big event, I knew the queues would be crazy so I went outside to help with the queues, I walked up and down making sure everything was ok, then I suddenly stopped in my tracks and had to double take what I saw, I saw a male in the queue peeing into a bin bag, I said "what do you think you're doing?", with that I had made him jump, he pulled away and suddenly his peeing turned into a fountain and shot over the barriers in my direction making me jump back, I saw his japs eye and everything, he tried to deny it while having pee all down his jeans.

one long hard night that I remember very well, I was on patrol when I walked around in the smoking area I overheard a female swearing at someone , I looked over to see it was a domestic with her boyfriend, I went and stood near so she could see me and hopefully she would calm down but she didn't so I switched on my bodycam to start filming it , one of her friends came over to me and I told it might be a good idea for her to have a word with her friend that she needed to calm down or she may have to leave , I thought her friend talking to her would be better then me going over, sometimes when people are angry they can get worse when someone with authority comes over and friends can calm them down , so I didn't want me interrupting to escalate the situation , I watched as her friend spoke to her , the girl then shouted in my direction " I don't give a fuck if I get kicked out ", let them fucking try and kick me out " , with that I calmly went over and spoke to her but she ignored me and acted like I wasn't there and kept pushing past me to carry on swearing at her boyfriend , I touched her arm to get her attention and asked her to come with me , she went mental trying to punch me , she was a very chubby girl with really chunky arms so I put her against the fence , her boyfriend then tried to grab me but my colleagues arrived just in time and took him away, the female was trying to push me off her with her weight but I managed to keep her against the fence ,

Sarah came and took one of her arms and I took the other , it was like the girl was possessed, some sort of inner strength, me and Sarah really had to put all our effort in this , we restrained males many times no problem but this girl was something else, the female kept throwing her body weight around and dropping her legs when we was trying to get her up the slope from the smoking area around to the front of the club, we finally got there, then we was trying to calm her down , telling her we are trying to help her and was trying to understand her behaviour but it didn't work, she was spitting , screaming , threatening , we warned her and told her we would be letting her go and to go home and not get herself further in trouble,

We then released her and moved back away from her , she went flying towards us trying to hit us so we restrained her again but had to put her to the floor , again she was screaming and making threats , I thought how has she got so much energy , me and Sarah was starting to run on fumes , we warned her again. , and that if she tried to attack us again she would be going back on the floor , and guess what yep ..she tried again so back to the floor for her , this wasn't easy , she kept throwing her weight about and wriggling dramatically , we was now at the point of calling the police but thankfully her friends came over , her friends were so different from her and was disgusted by her behaviour and kept apologizing to us for her.

We advised them to try and take her away or we would have no choice but to phone the police and that she might be arrested, so we let go of her while she was still on the ground and let her friends take over , she got up and ran at us but her friends managed to get hold of her and drag her away , her boyfriend ended up carrying her away as she kept trying to come back , me and Sarah was knackered from that and had to have a drink and fag break to recover .

most shifts at sometime in the night I would go and find Sarah for our nightly catch up, I'd find her and say " you ready for a chat?" , she would always reply " bare with I need a sip" while pointing a finger into the sky , it was a nightly tradition and she would need a sip of drink before we had a fag and a catch up , we would chat about staff performance, any issues I'd have down stairs and things I would run past Sarah before doing certain things or make changes.

The only downside in our team was our poor performing cctv operator, I was used to our top girl we had when I worked for the last company, we had a guy called Dean, he worked full time like me and worked up there with us in the evenings just like I did, he used to fall asleep in the camera room.

 I have empathy if he had debts to pay off or was struggling and that's why he did so many hours but going to sleep was taking the piss and putting people at risk but I think because he had worked for the company a long time and helped them out a lot that they turned a blind eye to it but I wasn't happy about it.

We used to have to radio cctv every half an hour after a toilet check to say it was clear and he was meant to reply back to confirm he had received the call like the old operator did but Dean never replied (maybe he was sleeping) so it used to confuse us and we would have to confirm with each other that our call did go through.. It made us think our radios had stopped working it was a right pain.

One night he was training a guy on cctv and it was about to be time for me to do a toilet check and suddenly he radioed me and said "can we start the toilet checks", what the f... we never normally hear from him the whole night and now he was showing off for the new guy.. Sarah followed me into the toilets, I turned to her and said" I ant havin that " (that's where the saying started), Dean left not long after and we had another guy that wasn't good at all and even caused a lot of issues for us at times, the thing is the cctv course doesn't make you good at the job.

I want to go back a little bit, I needed to start looking for a full-time day job, the days where gone where I would have five to six shifts on the door, I think a lot was to do with student fees increasing to nine grand a term, over time cut backs was slowly happening , so I spent nine months looking for a job, I applied for so many but never heard anything back from anyone, not even one interview, then a new female started on the door with us called Laura, she worked in the day time for a security company in retail, she had been a store detective for quite a few years for them, she told me there were looking for part time staff, I said I was very interested and she put my name forward and not long after I got an interview.

I was offered an eighteen hours a week, so that worked well with my door work, it took nearly two months to go through the security checks then I started, not long after a guy got sacked from the local store near me and my hours increased to twenty seven hours, I worked with two other guys there that was on full – time hours, Ganj and Jay.

These two guys hated each other and refused to speak to each other, Ganju was a guy in his fifties and wasn't a nice guy, on my first shift there he said "I don't know why Terry (our boss) asked me to show you around and show you what we do, I don't get paid for it so I'm only going to show you the basics the rest you will have to work it out yourself.

He hardly spoke to me when I worked with him, he would stand at the front of the store chatting away to someone on the phone, no idea what about as it was in his own language.

Now jay was awesome , lovely guy , was happy to help me and he was so good at catching people, I wish I got to work with him more but he got a job in London being a manager for a small team. Ganju put in a transfer to another store as he refused to work with Jay, He didn't know jay was leaving for another job and I asked Jay not to say anything till Ganju moved store.

I got one of the full-time position and the rest of the hours was covered by random guards, some was awful, we had one guy called Mark he was so little everyone thought he was about twelve years old on work experience, he was a nice enough lad but talked so much rubbish, he told lots of members of staff that this job was just for pocket money as he looked after famous people, he said he always looked after Tulisa the singer/rapper , he wasn't great at catching shoplifters, I really don't think the job is for him to be honest, he ended up being removed from the store , then a friend of Ganju called Baj came and joined us full-time, why they employed him I haven't got a clue, he didn't speak English and certainly didn't understand but I think a lot of the language barrier was exaggerated so he could do the bare minimum work.

My first catch was a young female university student, she had a fabric bag on her shoulder and was putting items into it, so I watched and saw her pick up steak, expensive orange juice and then random food items and put them into her fabric bag, she went to self-scan and I noticed she didn't pull out the steak or the orange juice, she put the fabric bag at her feet, scanned the other items and put it in a carrier bag then put that bag into her fabric bag.

I went to the front door and waited for her to leave, I stopped her and asked her to come back inside which she did, we went out the back to one of the rooms where she admitted she didn't pay for some items and there were more items she hadn't paid for which I hadn't spotted, in total it was about thirty pounds worth, she was given a banning letter by the manager and asked to leave the store.

My second catch was a woman in her forties, she put a four pack of beer in her basket then walked all the way back to the front of the store near the customer toilets , she picked up the beers from the basket, put the empty basket down and took the beers into the toilets, she came back out, the beers had disappeared most likely she had put them in her handbag, she then went and selected one banana and went and paid for it, I waited by the door, stopped her and went through the same procedure of recovering the item, getting her details and banning her from the store, I still didn't really feel good enough to do this job but I kept trying .

Our main job at the store was to deter we didn't have to get arrests if we got deters.

The deputy manager there Diana was a scary woman but a great one, I would say she was one of the best managers I have ever worked with and she always gave me great support.

The first time I did a stop with Diana was when one morning I was standing at the front of the store and I spotted a male in the distance walking through a closed check out with a carrier bag that was full, so I went and checked cctv and spotted the male walking around putting items into his basket he then walked past the tills picking up a carrier bag, goes down an aisle where I can see him on camera concealing the items from the basket into the carrier bag, he then walks out without paying, I showed the footage to Diana who told me to ring her when I next see the male in the store .

I spotted the male in store a few days later, I called Diana and she went and followed him, he noticed this and went and paid for his items at the till, me and Diana waited outside for him, where she stopped him and said "we are refusing your right to shop in here as we do not like your method of shopping, I know what you have been doing and you have been getting away with it for a lot longer then we know about, please don't come back ", the male agreed and left, I thought the way she phrase it was brilliant.

My next catch was when a member of staff was suspicious about an older male who came in the store early in the mornings, he would just appear from an aisle and walk past the checkouts with a carrier bag but would never buy anything, so with the date and rough time the member of staff gave me I check the cctv to see who it was, it was a man in his fifties, I printed off a picture and kept looking at it so I got his image in my head.

The following morning I was stood at the front of the store and saw the male enter, he went and picked up a newspaper then walked to the back of the store, picked up another item then took a carrier bag out of his pocket and put the item and the newspaper in the bag.

I walked to the front of the store and called Diana who came down to assist me, where we stopped him and asked him to come back in the store, we went to the training room where he admitted he didn't pay for the items, Diana wanted the police called (it was only for a £1.50 stop) but he pleaded with Diana saying his son was a police officer so she just decided to Ban him.

I was approached by the general manager and he told me that they was missing loads of grey goose vodka and believe it has been stolen, so I went back on the camera and watched where it was on the shelf, I went back on loads of days of footage till I found a young male late in the evening picking up five bottles of them and on camera I saw him put them in his backpack and then he walked out the door without paying so I finally found who was taking them.

I printed off a picture of the male and showed it to my colleagues, mark understood, but Baj, it took a lot of explaining but I don't think he understood anything I said, we were all on a rolling rota so we would all take it in turns doing mornings and late nights, so it was them on late's that week and I was really hoping they would catch the male.

I was still doing three shifts a week on the doors while I did my full time day job, I couldn't give it up as I had progressed and enjoyed the job. A lot of brand new doorman where now coming here and I started to train them, spend time with them and help them grow as doormen, I would even get to work early after some guys asked me if I would help them by showing things to help them, I really enjoyed it and it was nice to see them grow in the job and my bosses liked it a lot and it was now expected of me, I spoke to one of the bosses about it and he said the idea was when the company expanded that I would be in a paid training position and that I would go around different venues and help people and train the new guys .

I felt like a new person (I liked this person) I finally wasn't being judged on my looks and that I was good at my job, finally after all these years of being treated like shit, I had finally earned my place and I was going to work my ass off.

This gave me more confidence in my day job, I needed to stop being negative about myself.

One of most challenging nights on the door was an event that was a RnB night and a lot of Londoners had come to it, halfway through the night I was downstairs standing near the bar, when suddenly about twenty guys started fighting, I called it three times on the radio, I tried to pull people apart but it was a bit impossible and the main fighter was a six foot guy built like a house , he was huge, I was still waiting for back up, when a female who knew some of them got in the way and she got punched and went flying, back up arrived and we managed to sort it , the female was taken to the incident room with a swollen jaw, we kicked some of them out, then some others was walking around the club trying to find them (what a joke), we was on edge for the rest of the night and the moshing to the music was insane and we had to make sure it was under control and no-one got crushed, at the end of the night we sorted out queues for the cloakroom and a queue to get out, but they was all doing what they wanted to do it took us a lot to control them, Helen asked a male to move away from the door, he pushed her and told her to "fuck off " a doorman called Ady went to restrain him and the guys friends jump in to get Ady off their friend, Helen called it over the radio and some of us went in to sort it out, Rachel was on the front door screaming down the radio "get the police, get the police in here now ", I managed to radio "stand down on the last do NOT get the police, I repeat do NOT get the police", if we had got the police in, it means we have lost control and it could have had serious consequences either it could of effected the clubs licensing or we could of lost the contract (it was really silly for Rachel to call that) it was a fight end of and we brought it under control.

Chapter 5

At the end of the night once everyone was out, we watched as the customers was surrounding the police vehicles (the reason why they were there was because of the night it was), smoking weed , sitting on the police cars, it was a joke.

At the end of the night we had a private meeting between us all and we all agreed on the same conclusion, we spoke to the club manager and we all agreed that if the club ever did that event again that none of us would work it, they never did have that night again, but other places in town did and had the same problems we did.

We had a new female join us called Lucy, she fitted in straight away and she had great experience from her last job so it didn't take her long to get the hang of things, she would help out on the door sometimes after she finished doing searches, Phil had gone home early one night so Lucy was on the door with Helen with help from the head steward, I brought this male up from down stairs but he had issues with me for bringing him up so I left Sarah and Simon to deal with him in the incident room.
I went to the front door to have a quick check and Helen had gone to get someone's coat for them, Lucy was covering the queue which was empty as we was near last entry and the head steward James was talking to a male, all of a sudden the male ran past James heading to the doors, Lucy had her back to him so she didn't see it, it flashed in my mind that I don't know why this guy was running in, was he trying to get to someone and assault them?, he ran towards me, now I'm five foot five and he was nearing six foot so as he ran at me I palmed his throat and grabbed his collar and brought his head down while shouting for Helen who was nearby and an experienced door staff as I caught a glimpse of James and Lucy who froze, Helen called it on the radio and Sarah and Simon came out and we put the aggressive male to the floor, it was seen when watching back on CCTV that Lucy when coming to help she bent down and placed the clickers on the floor (please don't judge that, she didn't want to damage them and was new to this job she's a really good door supervisor) this lead to her nickname ' clickers'.

I enjoyed nights where we would have a famous act on, the thing that was a pain was the acts would always be brought through a side fire exit, rather than through the back where they could go straight into the green room, but the problem was there was no path way, just a steep bank and no lighting so I did understand why, it was just a pain as we would need quite a few door staff to escort the act from the fire exit to the green room and it would take at least a minimum of five as we would have to get them through a busy crowd to the back area, but it was fun , then I would need two staff for the front of the stage which were the normal positions anyway , then one for each side of the stage by the steps to stop anyone going past the barriers onto the stage.

Then there would be me and my second in charge and two others , then when the act went on stage I would monitor the crowds behaviour and if all was ok the four of us would leave the stage leaving the other four there, but it would depend on the behaviour of the crowd.

We had one famous R and B act on one night and we all stayed on the stage due to the moshing and people pushing, as well as looking into the crowd we would check the people near the front and make sure they were ok, , I spotted this guy who was very close and against the barrier, I went over and spoke to him a few times to see if he was ok or see if he wanted to get out but he said he was fine , I got staff to get a few jugs of water and some cups to give to the front of the crowd, the act was on stage for about twenty minutes and it all went ok and as soon as the act left I went back over to the male to see if he was ok, he wasn't and was unresponsive to me , clinging to the railings , I called over a doorman and we lifted him over the railings and took him out the back then out the back fire door to try and cool him down, he managed to get his breathing under control and we was fine after a while , but it just shows you one of the things that could possible go wrong, it happens at big concerts so it's very likely to happen at smaller venues.

I remember my parents telling me that in the mid 80's when they went to a Bruce Springsteen concert and they were near the front and had to be lifted out by the security as they was being crushed and that always stuck in my mind, as the saying goes expect the unexpected.

So the famous people I have met, Dizzie Rascal at a university ball, he fell of the stage and hit me with his microphone and landed on my colleague there's a video clip on youtube of that.

Leathel Bixxle, he was a really nice and down to earth guy, Dick and Dom, I wasn't a fan of there bogy/snot act but they were lovely guys.

Two girls from sclub, very nice..really enjoyed their music.

Do you know who were the stuck up assholes?, it was the ones from the realities shows, right up themselves, the famous ones were the most nice, strange init.

We caught two acts doing drugs back stage at different clubs, they was quickly kicked out of the place and not paid for coming, zero tolerance on that, I won't mention who they were.

The nicest person was Dj Westwood, he could of left after his set but he stayed met people, posed for photos and gave loads of stuff out, he was a dimond.

So other acts include, h20, Kano, Bucks Fizz , Miss Dynamite, Vicky Jackson aka number one pink impersonator, Professor Green, Titchy Strider, Diversity, Steve Mcfadden, The Chuckle Brothers, Matt Willis, 2 guys from Blue, East 17, Jason Donavon, all of them are lovely.

I should really talk about discrimination, I never saw or heard door staff being racist or homophobic to anyone, or it certainly never happened in front of me, I did get falsely accused of it many times when people didn't get their own way, my first memory was when I got called to take out a drunk female, I went to look for her and finally found her leaning against a wall kissing another female, I disturbed them and I could see the drunk female and she was wasted , I said to her friend " I'm sorry to disturb you, but your friend has had too much to drink and needs to come with me ", the girl was not happy with this and kept saying shes "fine"(my most hated word, I'm fine or there fine when they truly are not) so I called over another doorman as the drunk females friend was getting angry , we managed to convince them to walk with us, the drunk female was falling all over the place so I took hold of her arm and guided her, he friend went mental and told me to get off her arm otherwise she will complain of assault, we got to the stairs and I said to the other female " can you at least hold her, shes very unsteady on her feet and I don't want her to fall down the stairs" she replied " I fucking told you she's fine ", the drunk girl really wasn't anyway we managed to escort the drunk female out but her friend wanted to speak to the manager , the manager called mark had already seen what had happened, the friend said " I want to make a complaint that my friend got kicked out coz the door staff are homophobic , mark replied " I'm sure it's got to do with the fact that she is drunk, the friend started shouting " she's not drunk she's fine this is homophobic abuse, mark said to me and another doorman " get her out", so that was that, the two girls was part of the university football team, I later in the night bumped into one of them who told me they was going to put in a official complaint of homophobia, I told her you got to do what you got to do.

Other door staff asked me why I didn't tell them that I was in fact gay, I said " why should i?", I had done my job correctly and that's all that matters why I inform them that im gay aswell, I never did hear anything about the complaint, it did piss me off a bit thou, but it's just part of the job, I got called racist loads of times though out my career on the doors, I would try to explain to some about the situation hoping they would understand but they never did, it just seemed to me that if they didn't get their own way the race card would come out, I remember working at a club where on Saturday's they would have a no- trainers policy, this night there was six black guys came up and they was told this and they started being rude and calling us all racist, one of the guys was kind of friendly so I tried to make him understand, he said to me that his trainers cost £150 I said it didn't make a difference and said if they went and changed into shoes then they are more then welcome to come in and that everyone inside are wearing shoes and that's the policy and it had nothing to do with race, he seemed to sort of understand but then one of his friends interrupted and said to him " don't talk to this white bitch come on lets go ", so after them unjustifiable calling us racist and me trying to be helpful and make them understand I get called a white bitch and being racist to me, joke ah?!

It did get to me sometimes, because I'm not racist and I would get annoyed with people throwing the race card around for no good reason, I leave it with those incidents of discrimination because I could write a lot.

Of course I've got to talk about injuries I've seen or dealt with, there had been quite a few, the stabbing that happened, and a few others I've already mentioned.

There was a girl that was being silly on the dance floor doing handstands, I warned her to not do it and that she could injure herself or others, I thought she listened but I went away and did a toilet check I was only a few minutes and when I came out a girl come running over saying that someone had hurt themselves, yep same girl she was trying to do a back flip and she landed on her face knocking her two front teeth out, silly girl.

Another when two guys were brought to reception, one had headbutted another, the guy that had been headbutted had been somehow butted in the mouth which left him with a bleeding wobble tooth and the guy that hurt him had quite a deep cut on his forehead from the guys tooth, while I don't condone what he had done, I did feel sorry for him, he was genuinely horrified at what he had done and was very angry with himself, he said he didn't understand why he sometimes get like that, it wasn't the drink he wasn't drunk or tipsy, he said he felt red mist come over and he just flipped like he would black out , after myself spending many of my teenage years with anger problems I could sympathise with him and told him he needed to get help maybe anger management, he agreed and thanked me for being understanding, I hope he did get help.

One night I had a later start at the club due to my day jobs finishing time so I had about twenty minutes to get from that job to this one, I got there, got all my gear ready and started work, within about fifteen minutes there was a radio call for a first aider to the stairs, I went and saw a guy led on the stairs , his body look all twisted and his neck looked at a strange angle I thought it was broken his eyes was open and no response I honestly thought he was dead, I called for Sarah and Helen to come, I put two doorman at the bottom of the stairs to stop people and direct them over to the other stairs and a guy at the top of the stairs to stop people there.

Helen and Sarah took over on giving the injured guy first aid, while I went outside to phone for an ambulance away from the loud music, I had to radio Sarah and Helen that I was on the phone to them and to reply through them so they would be ready with questions that would be asked, despite how serious this situation was, the useless cctv operator wasn't paying attention and radioed " I'm just phoning for an ambulance now", I replied " stand down I'm on the phone to them ", I carried on replying to questions with the operator on the phone then came on the radio from cctv " I'm on the phone to the ambulance they are asking what has happened what shall I say?", I repeated the same as before and asking him to keep the radio channel clear, he then radioed the same again, I said to one of the guys on the front door " please go in and speak to him as he's obviously not understanding, thankfully he stopped radioing, the injured guy's breathing became shallow and at one point we thought CPR was needed , the ambulance came and it took a while for them to sort him out on the stairs.

While they was doing that we got a few of us in position to clear an area near a fire door , where we was going to escort the paramedics too, we had a few issues with the brother whom was trying to get to him, which is understandable.

Once they got him in the ambulance it took a while to get him stable, I think his body had gone into shock, the brother kept asking us how long it was going to be till they was leaving as he wasn't allowed in the ambulance while they was sorting him out , we told him we wasn't sure, he said he was going back inside the club to use the toilets, about twenty minutes later the paramedics came and asked if the brother was still going with them, we went looking for him and we couldn't find him anywhere, the ambulance moved to just round the corner and they had to stop again, we throught ' that doesn't look good', we found the brother, and guess what we found him dancing with some female , I couldn't believe it, his brother was seriously injured and he was behaving like that it even took some persuasion for him to come to the ambulance.

We finally established everything that had happened, he had been sitting on a ledge where people put drinks, behind the ledge was the stairs leading down to the bottom floor, a friend of his had been joking around and grabbed the guys legs lifting him backwards through the back drop curtains and going fifteen feet down landing on the stairs, I have actually seen the footage and its one of the worse things I've ever seen.

So the brother finally left with the ambulance then we had police on site, the stairs and the area where it happened still had to be closed off in case the male died, the police hung around until they heard of his condition, it was a few hours later that we heard back and surprisingly the male was fine, no injuries, probably because of his level of intoxication, like have you ever heard of drunk people that get hit by a car, sometimes they have no injuries because there body is relaxed, as when we are of sound mind, we freeze and we go stiff, so he was very lucky and the police left, but the club had to board up the wall between the stairs and the upper floor, we also had to have a steward to make sure nothing like that happened again, the male came into the club a few weeks later he didn't acknowledge us, no thank you or anything, he even had the cheek to go behind the bar and steal a pint of beer.

The incident didn't affect me but it did Helen for a while of him lying there eyes open , not moving like he was dead.

I didn't think about the effect on the young doormen till Helen mentioned checking in with them and making sure they were ok, I was kind of use to serious incidents so I didn't really think, we checked on them and they were ok, the club was really good about it and thanked us, they said they watched the footage of the incident and saw how horrific it was and said that if anyone needed counselling they would be willing to pay for it, I thought that was really nice of them as they didn't have too.

We was a solid team apart from cctv, we all knew what we should do, no one panicked, we was a great team, I couldn't of been prouder of them all.

We had quite a few door staff from eighteen to early twenties, they was very disciplined, mature and hard working for their age which was great to see, not like some of them you see now days, when I was eighteen when it was rare for females the guys had to be a certain size to get work or be accepted, not that size really means anything while it's a possible great deter , but it doesn't necessary mean a great doorman.

I have seen it for myself many times, at a club I worked at in town we had a guy join our team part-time, he was a really nice guy, he was quite a hence guy , he worked out a lot , he was also a part-time fire fighter, his position was by the dance floor but every time we had a a big kick off and we ran there he was nowhere to be seen till after the fight was over, he didn't last long with us, then with the last door company that used to slag off the other local company calling them idiots and bullies and they would always go on about customer service and not being aggressive and violent, then we had a guy join us aged about twenty , he was around six foot five, stocky not muscly, he wouldn't listen to what people were saying to him and would do his own thing, I would say to him ' do not go into a mosh pit, if there were an incident the guys was trained by me to go in , in a line holding onto each other from one side coming out the other side for their own safety but he thought he was too big to follow rules, I used to say to him " please stop doing that, you're putting not only yourself at risk but others and also it's not a good example to the others, he still kept doing it, thankfully he got moved into town to take advantage of his build, but his mentality was all wrong, and hadn't had time to grow and lose his arrogance or be around people that would have been a good influence on him.

 I had heard he would threaten customers, he also ended up breaking someone's wrist by being too rough, I had witnessed him deliberately slam a door into a group of people on purpose , another time he was escorting a male out and he said to the male " if you don't fucking shut up I will break your wrist", great customer service ah!?, I think people forget that if a customer is being abusive and you're abusive back you haven't got the upper hand you are just as bad as them, I think he thought he was being a big man behaving like that, so all that was happening and he hadn't had his badge for long he got made up to be head doorman at a top place, everyone was in a up roar about it , the ones that I had trained and they had worked there asses off for years becoming great doorman were really disheartened and pissed off about it , I agreed I couldn't back up or defend their decision as everyone had seen his bad violent behaviour , I couldn't really understand it myself , and as I said before it goes against everything they had drilled into us to behave while working for them of course some brown nosier told the office of what I said and I was pulled in, I told them what I thought , that a doorman who was a thug who had broken someone's wrist they said they sort of understood but the manager at the place wanted a really big guy on the door apparel which I sort of understood but the whole thing pissed off nearly everyone that worked for them, it didn't last long, not for his behaviour but probably due to lack of experience, but it still made the other staff restless.

So back to the store, the young male (grey goose thief) kept coming in during Baj shift and had stolen in total fifteen bottles so far , mark nearly caught him but did the procedure all wrong, he saw the guy put the vodka bottles in his bag but instead of waiting for him outside, he escorted the male to Diana, Diana asked the male to open his bag which he refused, they didn't have no choice but to let him leave, I don't understand why mark didn't wait for him outside, he saw the selection and concealment , I think it was the fact that he was too scared to do the stop by himself.

So on my next night shift I let the managers and staff know who to look out for, it got to half an hour before the store closed when the manager Louise said to me " it doesn't look like his coming in tonight " and with that I looked up to the alcohol aisle and saw the male, Louise said she would watch him as she was in her normal clothes , she phoned me to say she had seen him pick up bottles of Jack Daniels whiskey and put them in his bag and he was heading for the front doors, I stopped him and brought him into the manager's office where he refused to open the bag and refused to talk to us, so we called the police, we wasn't waiting long for the police to turn up, the police officer opened the males bag to find five bottles of Jack Daniels and also inside was a foil bag, which stops door alarms going off, he was arrested and also charged for a few other thefts from our store and received nine months in prison , I was proud of myself it was my first big stop.

It was hard to catch certain people when they knew I was watching, so it was handy when Laura came in, I would give her details of certain people, or if I see them come in I would ring her then she would catch them concealing items and I would help her stop them, it was fun when she was in, we were a team, the other guards was useless.

Laura came in one morning and we tried to get catches but nothing was going on, we was getting to the point of giving up and getting our redbull drinks and going for a smoke when I spotted this female with a trolley, she had two big bags in the trolley and was putting items in them, I phoned Laura to keep an eye on her , it was quite a busy day and the queues at the tills was quite long, we ended up losing sight of the female and suddenly she was at the kiosk buying a lottery ticket, we and Laura said to each other there is no way she has been through the tills that quickly when it's so busy , so we stopped the female as she walked out and took her to the back office, she admitted that she hadn't paid for the shopping and tried to say she was in a rush and had to go and pick someone up from the airport, I believed she had done this before , she didn't look nervous as she left without paying, and she had time to get a lottery ticket, the value was about £150 , we didn't bother calling the police and just banned her.

It was still a bonus for us even if we just banned her , as we had her details we would send it off to the correct department and they would be sending her a civil recovery letter which would be a fine around £150.

I remember a kids mum phoning up once to complain about this fine, her daughter had tried to steal a bottle of alcohol that was around £5 , so she didn't understand why the fine is £150, she was told that regardless of the amount stolen (also moaning that we got the bottle back) it's a set fine, it's for administration and cost for security.
The daughter was eighteen so if she had been younger she wouldn't of done , I don't remember the incident I think it was one of the store detectives catch.

Obviously there has to be some kind of consequence for people's behaviour but one that I can never understand is homeless or drug addicts, when they go to court for shop lifting they end up getting a fine instead of jail time , now what is the point of that??, they can't afford the fine so to pay it they would have to shoplift so I find that totally pointless .

So when I first started at the store they got a few weeks jail time, so we wouldn't see them for a while and even after they came out it would be a good few months before they tried to come back in so we didn't have to worry about them, then suddenly they would be in shoplifting to pay for the fine they got for shop lifting in our store in the first place, not a deterrent at all.

The only good guard was called Eric that was good in the early days, he ended up leaving because our manager would keep making him do all the overtime when he didn't want to, he felt pressured, he was only meant to be doing twenty seven hours but would end up doing fifty plus and that's not including the door work he did so he took a transfer, that was a shame I liked working with him.

Baj was a pain to work with I had to deal with all the situations as he didn't speak English, none of the staff would bother taking incidents to him they would wait for me to be on shift, he never caught anyone, he would make up deters and lie and put them on the report forms.

The one time when it was beyond a joke with him was when me and Laura had an incident before he came on shift, Laura spotted a male putting a bottle of Jack Daniels down his trousers, I knew she was about to stop someone by the way she walked, she pointed to a guy that was walking out of the door, we stopped him and he said he was going to stab us, so for our safety and everyone's that was about we continued to restrain him, he started throwing himself about and we took him to the floor, we had him pinned on his back with his arms out stretched, I noticed in his hand there was a syringe but it had no needle on the end so I thought to myself that it was a scare tactic, the police came and arrested him, me and Laura then went outside for a cigarette, I was standing there chatting when I looked down and saw the needle sticking out of my leg, I was in shock, I took the needle out and put it in an empty cigarette packet and Laura went and called the police to update them with this.

I went and spoke to one of the store managers who told me to go to the hospital straight away, I called my boss who was now Greg and he agreed with that, Baj just came on shift and I tried to explain what happened, I told him three times then I gave up, I asked him to burn the cctv footage for the police and he refused (I don't think he would of done a decent job anyway as he can't understand) so after going up the hospital and having my blood taken to test it I had to return to the store, outside of my working hours to burn the footage.
 I then got a call from the hospital saying they think I should go back up there to get some tablets that can stop me from getting HIV, so I had to go all the way back up there.

The police came to the hospital to get a statement, I didn't get home till nearly midnight and had to be back at work for seven in the morning, I hadn't had time to eat during the whole day.

I had to wait months for the results but luckily it came back all clear, the guy pleaded guilty and got two years in prison, somehow it ended up on the front page of the local newspaper, I believed my ex employer told the newspaper about the incident.

Back around this time we didn't have a cctv desk at the front of the store, so what I used to do if I thought anyone was acting suspicious I would write the time and details in my pocket book and would check the cctv footage when the next guard would come in.

This day I was stood at the front of the store when I noticed this female and she had come from round the back of the aisles heading towards the front door, what really made her stand out was that she was wearing massive sunglasses that nearly covered her face and a female fishing hat pulled down over her head, she was carrying a carrier bag and it was rammed full but I couldn't tell what it was, I thought ' great she's definitely taken something' so I wrote it down in my book, then within twenty minutes two elderly ladies went to the customers service desk to say their handbags had been stolen.

I had a feeling straight away that it was the woman I had seen, I radioed on the town radio about what had happened, I was directed to our watch website and to look at a certain persons profile and to confirm if it was the same woman I had seen, I radioed that it was the woman in the picture, the police knew of her and found her at home with the handbags in her car boot, thankfully all the contents was still in there, they also found another fourteen bags in her possession so she was arrested for sixteen handbag thefts, so that was a good job.

Another shocking incident with Baj's behaviour one afternoon, I had just paid for my shopping after finishing my shift and was just about to leave when a woman came running in saying a wasp had just stung her son and wanted to warn us that the wasp had now entered the store (I know right!) anyway I left and went home,
I came back to the store the next day and a member of staff called Dave told me the rest of what happened after I left the day before, Dave was coming into work and had been walking across the car park when he saw a guy jump out of his car with a baseball bat and started smashing up his own car.

Dave went in the store and found Baj and told him what was going on, but Baj's reply was " I is busy catching fly ", while he was rummaging in the apples, ten minutes later Baj went up to Dave with some tissue in his hand and said proudly " I caught fly " (honest to god that happened).

The deputy manager Diana got Baj removed from the store as he was utterly useless when incidents would happen, he would just stand there grinning, but he still came back from time to time to cover shifts.

Ion then came and joined us, a Romanian guy, he was nice and spoke perfect English it was nice, but me and him had to make up the hours as we was still a guard down and we was also told there was going to be more hours for the store so we needed two guards, I got talking to a doorman that I have known for years and he was interested in joining us called Kyle, I knew he would be good at the job and I was looking forward to working with him.

But first an Egyptian guy called Maat was going to be joining us, our new boss Mick said he was ex-army and had loads of experience in retail security; I was really excited about this and thought finally we are going to have a great team at this store.

On Maat's first shift I showed him around, showed him our duties and we got chatting, he told me a bit about his life in the army and his family, he seemed nice.

A few days went by and it seemed Maat could no longer understand or speak English, the only conclusion I could come to about this was he was lazy and wanted to do the bare minimum, how can you go from talking English fine to not being able to, I thought great he is going to be fun to work with.

Kyle came and joined and it was like a bit of fresh air, Ion was getting moody as he was getting pissed off with Maat not doing his daily duties and Ion had to do everything on their shifts.

I spoke to our boss Mick about Maat, who was shocked that Maat was pretending that he didn't speak English and him not doing his work, he said he would speak to Maat about it, Maat improved for a couple of weeks but went back to his old ways.

Mick made me acting team leader, which was brill, I wanted to learn more so I started doing our store rota.

Things were getting worse with Maat we had so many complaints about him from members of staff for refusing to help, or if they asked him to watch someone, he would wave them away with his hand and say no.

Maat would also never do the guarding duties he would leave it for the rest of us to do them, he would come in late to work, go home early, go for loads of breaks but I had enough of complaining it just wasn't getting anywhere, but it was getting so stressful trying to look after the store when he was on as well as doing other duties that we had to do.

It was an even worse day if I was on shift with both Maat and Baj (yep he came back to the store) (so both spoke no English well Maat pretended he didn't) everything I had to deal with it was beyond a joke.

I was just finishing my break (which was rare for me to have as normally I didn't have time working with these idiots) when I got a call to the front of the store, where this guy in his early fifties had his top off and was shouting and swearing, Maat and Baj was just stood there staring into space not even trying to talk to the guy, what had happened was the guy came into the store without a top on (its policy that customers must wear tops) and both of them decided to go and speak to him about it (it shouldn't of been both of them and they most likely came across rude with their lack of English skills) the guy had said no and both Maat and Baj decided to follow the male round the whole store no wonder the guy was pissed off, but now they did sod all to calm the guy down and was just staring at him, which left me trying to deal with it, the guy made threats at me and started filming me on his phone, you could tell he wasn't a nice guy anyway but it didn't help with the other guards behaviour .

They were both awful in dealing with anything, I was always called off my break to deal with incidents because they weren't capable, I got called down from my lunch one time when two taxi drivers were nearly fighting in the car park, when I got there manager Diana turned to Baj and told him to go away as he was useless, he was just standing there watching the fight happen, by the time I got there another member of store staff sorted the situation out.

It was alright for these guys, even though we are paid for our breaks so we are meant to deal with situations if needed but when these guys went for their breaks they would go and sit in their cars and turn their radios off so their breaks were never interrupted and they got away with it.

I was always coming into the store every day and getting complaints about the other guards and having to deal with thefts that happened on their shift.

We had another guy covering an evening shift called Raj, I came in the next day to a complaint about him, two customers had gone to the customer service desk to tell staff member Claire that they had spotted a known shoplifter in store filling a sports bag full of alcohol, Claire phoned Raj and explained what was happening , he asked if there was any shouting, she replied no and he said he wasn't coming down then, we lost £400 of alcohol, I spoke to him about it and he denied Claire told him, I know Claire and she would of, another guard just being lazy and not doing anything, so muggings here had to look back on cctv, burn the disc and contact the police about the theft.

I really think door work kept me sane, I was working loads of hours doing both jobs.

The problem I had was I was too passionate about my job, no matter what job I had I always gave it a hundred per cent, I cared too much, unlike these guards that just did as little as possible I often wondered, didn't they feel embarrassed that managers and staff thought they was useless I know I would if it was me.

I was finishing a day shift at the store then I had to go and work at a big event, I put on an old pair of boots that was a bit too tight as my other boots had a hole in it and as I was in charge of an area I didn't want to look trampy with a hole in my boot, I would come to regret that later, it was the second time I was a supervisor at a big event so I was going to work my ass off, I covered the burger van, exits, rides and the toilets, I made sure everyone in my team got a fifteen minute break and fag breaks, it went well, one of the concerns we had in our area was a few people trying to climb in but we caught them, one incident which was quite amusing , we saw a male climbing over the fence behind the toilets, me and the response team went to find the male upside down in a stingy nettle saying to us " I'm so sorry , please get me out, please please".

I could now feel my feet hurting so much to the point I was almost limping but I tried hard not to show it, I didn't have time for a break myself but as long as the staff on my team was happy that's all that mattered.

Back at the store It was suddenly busy for me catching shoplifters without the help from the other guards, I caught a female one evening, around early twenties, I could see she was drunk, she was walking around just putting things into a carrier bag and walked out, of course I stopped her.

 Another time I was told by a customer that a woman was filling up her own fabric trolley, she was with another female who had a basket, I watched them go to self-scan and they paid for items that was in the basket but didn't get anything out of their own trolley, so I made it obvious I was watching them, they then went to another till and emptied the fabric trolley, it was around forty pounds worth, they didn't come back to the store after that for nearly a year.

One boring afternoon I had a female customer come up to me saying she had been on self-scan and had left her purse and now it had gone and had not been handed in, I took her details and told her I would look into it

So I had the time of when the female was at the till, I looked and noticed a smartly dressed female go to the till, she picked up the females purse that she had left behind and she put it in her little trolley , I carried on watching and noticed her behaviour was quite strange, I went and got this females shopping receipt printed off so I could check with what I saw, I noticed she had quite a few bottles of wine but there was none on her receipt , it seemed she was weighing them on the scales as bananas , some bottles of wine she was just leaving them in her trolley, she didn't pay for all her food shop but I couldn't see what the items were so I just concentrated on the bottles of wine, I burnt the cctv for that incident but decided to investigate further as I believed that this woman was possibly doing this with the wine for a long time, so as her daughter was always with her in her school uniform I believed she would come in after school had finished , I checked where the wine she choose was on the shelf and it was under a camera, I checked back over the days and noticed she came in most day after school time , done some shopping pick roughly four bottles of wine and did the same thing at the checkout, I printed all the receipts off and the receipts would show she was only spending a maximum of around ten pounds, so she was stealing a lot with the unknown food and wine which was around seven pounds a bottle, so I burnt off all the cctv, done all the statements and printed all of the receipts , I then kept a eye out for her .

The following day I spotted her, watched her on cctv at the self-scan and she did the same thing, I waited for her to leave the store , I stopped her and asked her to come back in, she acted all normal, we had to wait for her daughter to come out of starbucks then we went to the back office , I said to her would you like your daughter to sit in another room with a colleague while we discuss, but she refused so I explained to her why I had asked her to come to our office, what I had seen on the cctv and about the purse, she admitted to it all apart from the purse, I didn't push it and explained it would be dealt with via the police, which I then called.

I asked her if she would like to phone anyone to come and pick her daughter up as there might be a possibility that she might have to go with the police , she refused, it was horrible to see that her daughter was getting so upset and distraught , we was waiting quite a while when she said she needed to pick her other daughter up from college, I said she would have to arrange something else as she would be able to leave , she then told me that her daughter a was type one diabetic and she needed to give her insulin , I did think to myself " well her daughter is around 16 and wondered why she couldn't do it herself " but it wasn't my place to say so I called the police to update them and hoping they would come quicker .

We had been waiting for just over a hour and due to her daughter being there and being so upset I didn't really want to hold them and longer, so I asked if I could photo copy her driving licence and I would let her leave , she agreed and then I left her go and of course I kept the shopping she didn't pay for .

I called the female who had her purse stolen and had said I had caught the person and am waiting for the police to make contact and she could pass my details on to the police and what I have said.

The next day the female came in , she said the police had called her and that a female had come into the police station with her purse saying that she had accidently picked it up thinking it was hers, everything was still in there, including the money which was a bonus, the female was very thankful for my help, least that was a good outcome .

The police came in later that day for all the evidence, but much to my disappointment they phoned me a few weeks later to say they was abandoning the case as the address on her driving licence was wrong and that she didn't live there and they couldn't trace her it was quite gutting as she had stolen nearly a thousand pounds within a month, most likely a lot more, who knows how long she had been doing it for .

Refusing people alcohol due to them being intoxicated was always a hard one, because of the chances of them kicking off which is high when they having been drinking already , I did used to dread it , we had old male in his fifties that was refused and he started to kick off demanding to speak to a manager saying that his doctor allows him and he needed it for the morning or he could die, shouting and swearing saying if he does die it will be our fault, he did leave but not before saying he will be going to the papers and his MP.

I came to work one day and got talking to a customer she asked if the other security officer told me about a trolley push she had witnessed , of course not it was Baj, I said no and asked what had happened, she stated she had seen a woman just walk out with a trolley full of stuff and didn't pay and she had told him but again he didn't really understand and just looked out the door, he didn't investigate or leave us a note for one of us to do it, she told me what day it happened and a rough time and I went and checked the cctv, and sure enough I found an elderly lady putting random things in her trolley as well as food and just walked out the door with it .

I couldn't really work out a amount but most likely one to two hundred pounds, I burnt the cctv and printed out the best picture I could of her for the other officers to see.

A week later I went in for my night shift and Adam told me it all kicked off in store as ion had asked a lady to leave who he believed was the woman who did the trolley push , this woman was about 20-30 years younger than the thief , the only thing that was the same was the colour of her hair, oh ion.. he's lucky the management didn't get rid of him , but they sent her a hamper and some flowers to apologise and that was that thankfully.

A few weeks later the right woman came in , I watched her out the back on cctv as I didn't want her put off, she did the same thing and left without paying, I ran out and caught her and brought her back in, it nearly all kicked off when she made a phone call and her grandsons came, I recognised them straight away they were also shop lifters and one of them was banned, thankfully they didn't kick off, as I told the woman that it would make things worse with them hanging around , so she called them and told them to leave and they did, I then got a call from the police which really pissed me off to say they wasn't coming as due to her age which was 78 that they wouldn't prosecute , she had all her marbles and knew what she was doing, it seemed her whole family did it , so we ended up just banning her, we didn't see her again, but did have to keep dealing with her grandsons for shoplifting .

I was amused sometimes with some shoplifters , I remember one eastern European lad, I don't know why I could just tell when they are up to something , he came in with a basket picked up a pint of milk and went down the alcohol aisle ,I kept peering round and he was picking up loads of £40 bottles and putting it in a basket and walked off around the store, I deliberately walked close behind him and he put down the basket and walked out of the store, I said to him " oi don't you want that alcohol " he turned round and shouted " fuck you" did make me laugh .

Self-scan is a big problem , I would say stores lose a lot of money each day through self-scan , a lot of people are like me and you and it starts with something innocently happening, they would most likely accidently didn't scan something , sometime, most likely thinking " oh that was easy " then

they start doing it on purpose saving themselves a bit of money and it continues from there, its not always people who look rough that do this, its people like me and you, people that you wouldn't think that would do it, people with good jobs , even well off people do it, it annoys me , that is one of the reasons why our food and drink go up, I should know , you think food just goes up because of inflation, well that's one of the reason but a percentage of it is to accommodate the amount of theft, I give you an example, right ! do you know one of the high theft items?, so razors, there is a well known brand that sells a packet of just the razor blades, in store cost is £25 pounds, now we was having a problem with a very high theft of them and I went to a managers meeting to discuss this and I was told the manager had spoken to HQ about this and the things we could do to lower the thefts, we was informed that the £25 packets, only cost them £3 a packet from the brand company and it was at that price to accommodate the high theft, so there you go.

some people say, the stores can afford it , its not like stealing from a person, I've had a few shop lifters tell me that, but as well as the inflation, they have to save money from somewhere when there is big losses and another one is they will cut back on staff it's a vicious circle.

What do I think is a big problem when it comes to theft, its people that are unemployed , and I don't mean the honest people, I'm talking about the people who use it as a life style and have no intention of getting a job, these are the people not necessarily stealing, some do , but they are the main customers of the shoplifter.

Shoplifters have told me they get given lists from people of what they want .

Anyway let's get back to it .

So self-scan, I got called over by a member of staff who pointed out a female who she believed wasn't paying for some of her items, the staff member had seen her before and was suspicious of her, so I watched her and she scanned a bottle of water, then she places two other items on the scales and started pressing the screen which means she's weighing the items as something instead of scanning them, she went to walk out and as she did I stopped her and asked her to come back into the store, she only admitted to what she did after I explained what I saw her do, before when we was walking to the office she was acting like she didn't know and kept asking me what was wrong , her receipt showed she had weighed the items as carrots, the amount was around forty pounds , she was banned from the store.

One day I was having such a boring day , trying to watch the cctv and spot someone shoplifting but nothing, I was almost about to give up and just go and chat to staff when I spotted a woman with a child looking at the toys and picked up a toy car (we had previously found lots of empty car packaging) so I thought I might as well watch, she ripped open the packaging and placed the car in the child's back pack and throw the packaging at the back of the shelf and walked off.

I went and got the packaging and spoke to the manager called mike , he wanted me to approach her with the packaging at the tills, I spotted her at a till with items on the belt , I went up to her and explained all, she agreed to pay but took all her shopping of the tills and was putting it back in her basket and said she wanted to walk around, most likely she had more stuff and wanted to dump it, I told her she must pay for the toy now, I saw she dumped a carrier bag under the till which I checked and found some of our store brand clothes inside which obviously she wasn't going to pay for either, I suspected she was the female I had spotted in the past trying to steal, I warned her that if she did this in the future that she would be banned.

I told mike what had happened and what was said and he was happy with that.

Some thefts were just so random, I watch a young guy pushing a trolley and he was with another friend that had a trolley, what made me watch him was that he had a big sports bag and he was carrying it on his shoulder, I thought it was strange because if it was me I would sling it in the trolley, so I watched him, I also noticed the end pocket on his bag nearest to him was open, so I thought hmmm maybe, his shopping in his trolley looked normal, meals and that, he walked down the confectionery aisle and he picked up some chocolate and put it in the open pocket on his bag, I wanted him walk around and he paid for his trolley items and was about to leave the store when I stopped him, his friend looked shocked and don't think his friend had a clue with what he did, he was a big lad and I was expecting him to kick off but he didn't, so his shopping came to £35 but the chocolate he stole came to £8, strange I know , he just said he was stupid to do it , he was banned .

Another time a woman in her 40's came in, the thing that made me watch was that she had put her carrier bag in her basket , she picked up a pint of milk and another item and moved the bag to put the items in, then she went down the confectionary aisle, she picked up a big bag of m&m's and put it in the carrier bag, I watched her at the till she didn't get it out , I banned her and made her pay for it .

Another quiet day and I was trying to keep out the way of an annoying guard that was at the front of the store who was refusing to share time on the cctv , so I sat out the back , I noticed a couple had come round the tills a strange way if they had just paid for the stuff in the trolley but I didn't have enough evidence to stop them, so I spent a while re-winding on the cctv, as they might have paid and went back down aisle to look at something, sometimes this happens, but they hadn't been to the till and I found footage of them putting all their items into shopping bags , it was annoying so I thought they would be back and hopefully I would catch them some other time.

It was about a month later on a Sunday they was back in, wearing the same clothes so It wasn't hard to spot them , they did there same routine , I called manager mike who stood with me out the back on cctv, as they got nearer the door, the male went to the kiosk and the female and trolley left the store , we ran to the front and waited for the male to leave and join her, we stopped them and brought them back in, she said she was trying to find her husband as he had the money, hmm well they wasn't heading back in the store when he joined her, I explained we know its not the first time and had saw them on cctv doing the same the month before.

We called the police and waited, the value of the theft was about £150.

 The woman asked for something to eat and drink as she was a diabetic, so mike got her a sandwich and a drink of water.

Not long later the female went mad and started to try and hurt herself with items she could find, and I had to keep restraining her and taking items off her, while her husband just sat there, she then began headbutting the table.

Thankfully the police turned up and seemed to be quite annoyed I had phoned them and just gave them a verbal warning and asked them to leave.

I tried hard tried hard to keep a good report with the police , I didn't call them unless the theft was of a very high value, or someone was being violent .

But it was hard with some of the other security officers, being aware of the cut backs on the police etc, also not wanting to waste there time, other then the situations stated above, we would just ban people , other security officers would call the police for a few pound theft, which was really embarrassing , I also had someone important mention that one of our non - english speaking officers we had in store one day shouting down the town radio " police come now (store name)", they replied " which one " as there was 3 of the same stores in our town, the guard just kept saying " you come now ", they ended up ignoring him, just these things could ruin the good relationship with the police, another example I was in store one day with baj , I think it was coming up for a bank holiday and the store was going to be closed the next day , I had to guard a member of staff while they was emptying and closing down most of the tills, baj came over and told me police was there wanting some cctv, I knew what cctv they wanted so I asked him to go to the office and get the discs that was on the computer keyboard and give it to the police.

I couldn't swap with him as he wasn't allowed to do what I was doing as he did it before and kept walking off.

He came back to me from the office confused, I had to write it down on a bit of paper " CCTV FOR POLICE " , I said find what this says on the disc that was on our keyboard in our office, I finished helping the member of staff and made my way to the front of the store to see a female police officer standing there, I looked over at the cctv podium to see baj standing there, I thought " you are joking me" I went over to her and she said she was there for some cctv, I asked if the other officer had not gone and got it, she replied that he didn't and seemed confused, I was so pissed off again I had to do everything even the most simplest things, I went to the back and picked up the disc that had " cctv for the police " written on it and gave it to the officer, again another embarrassing moment, it would get to the point when police wouldn't come in unless myself , ion or Adam was in, like if I spoke to a officer on the phone and they had to come in and get some cctv they would ask when I was in next so they could get it then, I don't really blame them.

Another one that people do a lot, is steal items then get a refund for it to get the money or store credit.

The first one I remember was when I got called over to the customer services desk, a female had got a refund on two electrical items with no receipt, so I check on cctv, yep the female picked up to store brand electrical items of the shelf and went straight to the desk and got a £100 refund, you may wonder why the staff allowed this, two reasons, number one.. you can get a refund without a receipt if it's a store brand only, number two , the staff are very good about not giving refunds if they are suspicious but managers would end up over ride them and allowing the refund saying " just this once" because they couldn't be bothered with the arguments, so you can understand why the staff would get annoyed with this when they have spent ages saying no for a manager to just go yes give them the refund , but obviously the staff member was suspicious so that's why she called me to check it out.

I saw the female once more a few months later trying to return expensive pans which would of totalled £150 so I stood right near her , she pretended she just wanted a price check, then left not before smirking at me the cheeky cow, I never saw her again but I'm sure she went to other stores.

I was told another time by a staff member that this female was kept bringing stuff back for a refund , a lot of the time it was stuff she had eaten and said it didn't taste right and would get a refund, I spotted her on cctv and suspected she was a student in our town from London.

She came in again for a refund with 4 pairs of leather gloves saying her name brought them for her but she didn't need them, so she got nearly £80 on a store card and went off and did a load of shopping with her refund.

She came in another day and I tried to watch her which was really hard , she walked around with a basket and choose a few bits went and paid and

I thought oh she's not doing anything today , then she went to the desk again, and returned two different hairsprays and got around £8 , I was so annoyed I didn't see this, I went to where they were on the shelf and there was one missing on each brand she returned, damn it ….

I put the word out with customer service staff to alert me if she tries to return anything.

A month later she tried returned with an expensive electric shaver nearly £100, the security tag had been ripped of the box and the receipt she had was not the original it was a duplicate receipt from the croydon store (in London) , what most likely happened with this is, someone brought it , got the original receipt and asked for a duplicate, returning the original shaver, then stole one, and now was trying to return it with the duplicate, we had to ask the store managers permission to refuse and speak to her about it , it took a lot of persuasion as the manager thought it was ok, but myself and other staff was kicking off with him and as he walked off to speak to the female we still thought he would allow the refund , but he didn't he refused and said she seems to be returning a lot of items every few days, thank god ! another one we never saw again.

It's bad when we really have to fight to stop a fake refund .

Some would still get through because of no support from a manager lets go through some stupid ones people have got away with .

1. A male complained the chicken he had brought tasted funny, he had no chicken, no packaging and no receipt and he got a refund
2. A couple who returned a opened pack of condoms and some lube, got a refund
3. A jacket that I saw myself that looked years old , covered in dog hairs and stunk of cigarette smoke , got a refund
4. Knickers that the female stated that had fallen apart, you could clearly see the thread had been unpicked , got a refund

Joke isn't it , I don't know if it's totally the managers fault, or there is pressure on them for keeping customers happy, as I know the store do as much as possible to avoid bad publicity.

We had one great female manager who didn't take no crap, one of the popular scam that people would do is this…, a guy come in saying two six pint of milk had leaked in his car and wanted the store to pay for a cleaning bill and would have pictures of the milk all over the car , she told him that she's not stupid and that he wouldn't be getting no money from the store and basically told him to jog on, brilliant, but it just shows the length people will go to try and get free money.

Sometimes we was fighting a losing battle with things, for example, during certain times of the year the store would have a sale on popular electrical items, one of them was dyson hoovers and they would put them at the front of the store and the team leader was meant to put alarm tags on it but never did as he was so lazy , so we would come in and spot these £300 hoover right at the front door where people could just lean in the door a steal one, so we would have to tag it despite we wasn't meant to, we would argue about couldn't they be moved to somewhere safer but the reply would always be, that the head office would want it there.

        They also put laptops out live (live means the item is in the packaging rather then a empty box) this time the alarm tag was put on but I showed them how easy it was to slip off, they didn't care and they wouldn't even put it under a camera so we could keep a eye on it, so six laptops was out and they was all stolen within a week, well…. We did tell them but they think they know better, so that was a £1800 loss with just them.

My favourite argument was with the expensive vodka at forty pounds a bottle we would get gangs in stealing it all, so the staff would put out ten bottles of each and they would be stolen within a few days, I tried to explain about just putting a card out for staff to go and get it if a customer wanted it but they said the store (brand) policy is to have the item there for customers to pick up themselves, but the problem was all the stores in our town was having the same problem with gangs stealing this vodka so none of the stores would put bottles out on the self , only an empty one with a card asking to ask a member of staff for the item, so the only place left for them to steal from was our store, so as well as catching a few of the gangs we had to wait for about six months and a five gran loss on them for the manager to finally agree to only put on bottle out , then the theft stopped .

As time went on when the department managers changed they didn't really care about tagging things we always went on and on about it, only a few staff members who was on different departments would do the tagging and the lazy ones didn't bother, which as soon as that would happen we would get a big spike in thefts .

Like the time they put out two grands worth of expensive perfume that they was meant to put in security boxes but didn't bother and in two days they was all stolen and the manager was kicking off about it , I told him 1. No security tags was put on them and 2. It was put on the self where the cameras didn't cover , we can only do some much , you could be patrolling somewhere and someone would come in a swipe the shelf and leave before you have walked back .

I used to clock some thefts that would be over within two minutes from the time the shoplifter had entered the store , pick up the items and leave .

Fast forward a bit I wonder how bad the store is now, since we all got made redundant, that store went from 3 guards a shift to one and that would only be in the store for 7-9 hours when the store is open for 15 hours and even then there is not a guard on every day, it was bad when we was there, bet it is amazingly worse, they have also cut back on staff so that's less on the shop floor, there was only a couple when I was there.

Where the store sits there is 6 areas they can exit the area outside , so very easy once thieves leave they have many areas they can escape too.

I would love to go back for a week and see how bad it's got, mainly because I'm nosy.

But I am glad I was made redundant as much as I got on really well with most of the staff and I did enjoy the catches , working with some of the other officers was too stress full and made me ill plus I did think to myself many times when I worked there that I couldn't stay there and be there when I was aged 45 and still be putting shoplifters to the floor etc .

I hear more and more guards getting injured, ok I was hurt with a needle and had very aggressive people to deal with but it seems things are getting worse because people know that the court sentences are getting lighter and the jails can't cope , shoplifters are taking more chances and are going equipped with weapons and are using them on guards, and as much as I think I was good at my job when incidents happen , having to deal with someone with weapons and knifes I'm not a ninja and I didn't wear a stab proof vest , I don't get paid enough for that and I wouldn't want to get seriously hurt.

Our company manager would say " don't put yourself at risk", but you are always putting yourself at risk every time you stop a shoplifter, so you won't know how bad the risk is until you have stopped the person and then it would be to late, so if you go with what they say and don't put yourself at risk you wouldn't be able to stop anyone and everyone would be walking out with items and I couldn't allow that.

Not being big headed I was quite savvy on how I stopped people and was quite careful with how I dealt with things and I think that's the best anyone can do when you do that job.

Anyway at the store We had quite an issue, a male would come into the store when we first opened in the morning and kept trying to walk out with a TV, luckily each time staff spotted him, it was an issue because the morning guards would keep coming in late for their shift, I managed to speak to the guy and ban him from the store which worked for a while. A few months later he came in and me and Ion went and spoke to him, tell him that he was banned, he demanded to see a manager, so we agreed to call a manager, I went to go and get the town radio from the cctv podium and as I looked back I saw the male kept aggressively getting in Ions face and as I walked over the male wacked Ion around the face with his basket, I shouted out to a member of staff to press the panic button and loads of staff came down, the guy went mental and we had to pin him to the floor, he was arrested by the police.

I tried to call our boss (who was now Terry again) to say Ion had been assaulted but no reply , I even left a voice message telling him what happened but he never bothered getting back to me about it or making sure Ion was ok.

When I was on a night shift I was walking around the store when I noticed two males down the bedding aisle acting strange and had a basket full of alcohol around three hundred pounds worth with a pillow set on top trying to cover it, I knew we wasn't meant to approach until they left the store, but I knew I wouldn't be able to catch both of them, so I knew I had to make something up so I approached them and said " Hi guys sorry to be a pain but due to the value of your basket we have a new policy that we will have to keep it at the till, till you have finished shopping and the items will be there waiting for you" they was so shocked they didn't know what to say and gave me the basket, I put it on a till and told them " guys it's on till fourteen when you're ready " I smiled and walked off, of course they wasn't going to pay and they left the store empty handed.

I compared their picture to another two males who had been stealing expensive alcohol and it was the same guys so I was well pleased.

The following day one of the lazy guards was on the cctv and I was there sorting out some paperwork when a customer came up to me to tell me a male was filling his pockets up down the make-up aisle, the guard wouldn't let me go on the cameras and said he would look (great he's useless) then I saw a known prolific shoplifter walking to the exit, I knew who he was and his coat was bulging and I could see a leg of meat sticking out his coat, I didn't follow the protocol but this was obvious , I stopped him and he said "have it back", handing me two legs of meat, I knew he had more, so I said to him that I wouldn't call the police but he needed to come back in, it took a while to persuade him but he came in , (no help from the other guard), when we got to the room I told him to give everything back, there was items coming out everywhere, loads of make-up, tins of coffee, meat, in total it came to nearly three hundred pounds, I was thinking about calling the police but I knew how useless this guard was and I couldn't trust him to look after the guy while we waited for the police (it has to be a male looking after a male) the guard Barji couldn't really speak English so I let the guy go, I couldn't risk it.

Working there was getting so stressful , I asked Ion to pull his socks up and support me, because he was kind of lazy but not as bad as the others, I was getting so worn out having to do everything, I had to rush about and do the jobs others wouldn't bother doing which was our daily duties, like checking the fire doors, checking stock was tagged correctly, checking cctv for theft, dealing with incidents on the shop floor, burning cctv for the police, making sure certain banned people didn't come in the store, staff searches as well as looking for shoplifters, while the other guards stood there doing nothing.

Kyle who I worked with on the doors came and worked with us which was nice, but he struggled working with the others too.

I could feel the stress, but I didn't know how bad I was getting, I had certain symptoms but didn't put them all together.

The only time I had a good time at work was when Laura was on shift at our store, as she was a store detective she would travel and work at many stores in the south east, we became good friends, we worked well together, around this time Laura was going through a hard time in her personal life, her and her partner had split and she was taking it hard, so she was finding it hard to get catches, you see store detectives have to hit a target each month or their job could be on the line, us uniformed guards only had to get deters, it didn't matter if we didn't get arrests, if we did then it was a bonus.

We had one crazy stop, Laura had seen a female de-tag a bottle of gin and put it in her coat, we followed the female outside and stopped her, the female kicked off and was throwing herself about as we restrained her, the female said "let me go and I will walk back in ", Laura started to agree with her and I said to Laura " I know this female and she will run ", but Laura believed her and we let her go, the female ran off, Laura ran after her and I joined and I saw the female swing the bottle at Laura's head and it just missed, the female then ran across the car park, I ran back into the store to get the town radio and came back out, I couldn't see the female or Laura , I was worried for Laura and i kept ringing her phone as I went through the car park to the field where I saw the female run too.
 there was a group of kids and they told me the female had run up into a gym fire exit, I went through and realised I was on the gym roof, Laura was nowhere to be seen, but the female was there going mental, I was

pissed and said " just give me the bottle back and you can go ", she did then ran off, I went back to the store and saw Laura was there so thankfully she was ok.

So I tried to help Laura by letting her have my arrests and there was a lot of them, sometimes it would be me that did all the work and brought people back in, it went on for months , she expected all my arrests which was now taking the piss a bit, our boss Terry said there was now a job offer as his assistant manager, Laura went for it and I was witness to her badgering Terry all the time about it, it seemed even though a lot of people was going for the job but didn't have a chance as Terry had already chosen Laura, and you know what?? As soon as Laura got this job she broke off our friendship and ignored me, what a bitch after all the help I gave her, I felt proper used.

Then this happened, I was sitting in our security room doing some paperwork, I looked up at the cctv screen and saw a male in the alcohol aisle loading up his basket with really expensive alcohol, I saw him take one of the bottles out of the box and dump it, I tried to radio Maat but no answer, I went out and went to where the male dumped the box to see if he had taken the security tag off as well , as I picked up the box, the male had walked back and clocked me he said "what are you doing?" I replied" just doing my job" and the male walked off, I knew Maat was on cameras at the front of the store (as that is where he stayed for his whole nine hour shift) I radioed Maat a few times, still no answer.

I decided not to follow the male and waited for him by the tills, I had a clear view up an aisle so if he walked pass the top area I could see him, I still kept radioing Maat but still no reply, all of a sudden the guy rushes out of an end aisle straight towards me shouting " I'm gonna knock you out", I was shocked by his behaviour, a male customer stepped in and said " don't talk to her like that " the guy throw the basket down and got in the customers face, I thought shit I'm going to have to restrain him in a minute , I radioed Maat again and still nothing, the guy left the basket and started walking backwards past the tills towards the front of the store while making threats to me and members of staff, we were now a the front of the store where I shouted to Maat " can't be bothered to reply then?", the male then turned and walked out of the store and I noticed something had been put up the back of his top.

I followed the male and he started running, I started running and speaking on the town radio hoping a police unit was near, Maat followed me, I dropped the store phone while running and shouted to Maat behind me to pick it up, I continued following the male, I spotted the male throw the item he had up his top over some bushes and ran off, so I stopped, I finished radioing on the town radio and asked Maat for the store phone, nope he didn't bother picking it up, so I asked him to go back to the store, picking the phone up on the way and speak to the store manager and ask if he wants to retrieve the item that was in the bushes as I couldn't climb over, or shall we just leave it, so off he went, it was now starting to rain.

Chapter 6

Ten minutes had past when the manager appeared, Maat hadn't explained things to the manager properly so he just came to see if I was ok, he wasn't happy that I had been waiting out there and he wasn't happy with Maat, see what had happened after Maat went back to the store to get the manager he decided to go and get a Starbucks coffee first, and the reason why he hadn't been replying on the radio is he put his radio back in the office an hour before the end of his shift, he also didn't pick up the store phone I dropped and when I went to look for it , it was gone, so despite saving the store three hundred pounds in stock , losing the phone cost two hundred and fifty pounds.

I was fuming and phoned our boss Terry to explain what had happened, ' and you know what?, he blamed me saying I shouldn't have put myself at risk, how the fuck did i?, and he kept going on and on that I put myself at risk with the guy when we was in the store, that was it I was burnt out after everything I had put up with, the next day I went to the doctors and explained how I felt and all the symptoms I was trying to cope with, lack of sleep, always tired, I noticed I just didn't care about things as much anymore and now I felt like I was in a dream state and sometimes I couldn't get my words out, I also explained what was going on at work and what I was having to put up with, the doctor told me it sounded like I was suffering from stress related depression and signed me off for a month.

I was so shocked... had I really got that bad? I cried my eyes out realising how serious things had got, I thought I would just get some tablets and get on with it, I spoke to Laura as she was now assistant manager to Terry, and she dealt with everything for me because I didn't want to talk to Terry, he had given me no support what so ever and blamed me for things that was wrong due to the other guards behaviour.

A few days later into my time off Terry had the cheek to text me asking me if I would do a statement on Maat's behaviour (I was now on depression tablets and they make you feel worse before you get better) I could barely hold a sentence together at the time, so I told Terry I wouldn't be doing a statement.

I continued to work on the doors as it wasn't door work that caused stress and I needed to get out of the house as much as possible and my door family was such a great support.

The one thing I wish the doctors would tell you when being prescribed tablets for this are for the first week, you have the shits, I mean constant. Couldn't trust a fart, ever, I did the whole Google thing and found out it was normal for a week or two till your body gets used to it but it was hard, I was asked by the door company I worked for if I would do a stall at an event for them, so I did, I enjoyed it but it was hard as I had to keep running to the toilets but I got through the five hours both days.

People don't understand when you go through depression that having people to speak to or just getting a nice text from people means so much and does help and I thank them for getting me through it, I was so scared I was going to feel like I did forever.

I had lots of down time to recover and it really geared me up to make some changes to get out of the store so I decided to finally start taking driving lessons, a lot of security jobs they want you to be able to drive, so that was my plan.

Our door company invited me and Helen to a head door/supervisors meeting, it was strange, I remember sitting there and my vision was so blurry I could see a strange halo around people, I sat there and started to panic a bit, I thought I was going to have a panic attack but I made it through, our bosses had asked me to be a trainer, I was so pleased and chuffed.

Kyle from the day job would message me saying it's the same at the store, and then near the end of my sick leave, Kyle said he was leaving as he nearly ended up like me due to the stress the other lazy guards brought.

It was a real shame Kyle was leaving he was really good and I enjoyed working with him and god knows who his replacement was going to be but I total understood, he went and worked for the door company we worked for in a full time position, so we was back with the useless gits when I went back to work then I heard another guard was joining us called Adam, he was brilliant and kept me sane, he was young at twenty three but was very disciplined and mature for his age (well when it came to the job) he hadn't been out the army long.

Adam was great at the job and very eager to learn, we became part of a good team, Maat got removed from the store so we was still one guard down so for a while we had various relief guards most of them was lazy and useless, then a guy called Paul came and joined us, he was in his fifties, he seemed ok to begin with but then he got his nickname ' the five second man' he couldn't remember anything, he was lazy and never did any guarding duties and kept saying he forgot to do them.

Paul would have a Bluetooth ear piece in and would listen to the radio during his shift because he said he was bored, what a joke, if he did the jobs he was meant to do he wouldn't have time to be bored , I once went to talk to him to tell him I had just heard from a guard at another store down the road that a known prolific shoplifter was on his way to our store, so I tried to tell Paul about it and that we had to keep an eye out for him right away, but Paul stopped me mid-sentence and said " can you wait ten minutes I'm just listening to my favourite radio program", what the fuck !, I just gave up with him after that.

I was the only guard that was licenced to go on the cctv but all the lazy guards would be on it for their whole shift, it wasn't my place to say anything and our boss Terry didn't really care (even through it's a criminal offence to be on the cctv without a badge) so when those guards was on shift I could never get on the cameras, what the hell did I pay three hundred pounds for it they was letting anyone go on it, I wouldn't mind so much if they spotted things but they would just be behind it so they can spend time playing on their mobile phones.

The store managers would always come to me to complain about the other guards and they was constantly complaining about Paul, there was an evening when he was on shift and a manager spoke to him about an incident but he said he was too busy 'what was he busy doing?' he was watching a film and eating popcorn (I know unbelievable ah!).

You may wonder why he was getting away with it, so let me explain a little bit, we worked for a security company and was contracted by the store, our boss Terry all he cared about was that the shifts were covered and that was it, it really didn't matter if you were good at your job or not and he would just sweep complaints under the carpet so to speak.

I know the store managers at the store complained to Terry about Paul but whether Terry spoke to him or not, I don't know as he never changed his behaviour.

Paul ended up getting another job and told people he was leaving because of me, a joke, not because he was lazy and had loads of complaints or anything, he shook my hand when he left saying "take care and I'm sorry we didn't always get on", I nearly said 'well if you weren't so lazy' but I didn't we was rid of him.

The next guard to replace him was Jason, I had high hopes for him as I had done a shift with him before and he helped me with a shop lifter with no problems, so after all this time I finally thought we had a whole decent team.

Jason did all of the guard duties that the old guards couldn't be bothered to do so that was a good start, he was mid to late forties and had been in the navy, he wasn't a talkative guy, everything was good until a member of staff pointed out something that I hadn't notice before,

 staff had spotted Jason picking his nose and wiping it through his hair, I was in shock and thought surely not, but others said the same thing and I spotted it on cctv, he would stick his finger right up his nose , have a good rack around then wiped it through his hair (now this was a problem for me, I had a thing about snot, it makes me feel very sick) I just ignored it as I know our boss wouldn't do anything about it.

Until one day when Terry came to visit our store and Adam told him about Jason's dirty habit and Terry didn't believe Adam as I hadn't said anything, I told Terry I didn't bother as nothing gets done about anything and that I just stayed out of Jason's way, but the store manager complained to him about it while he was there so he had to believe us.

A few days later Jason came on shift and Terry must have spoken to him, he was cleaner, had a haircut and was no longer wiping snot in his hair, so for the time being things was fine and no complaints.

Jason went on holiday and we had a guy called Mo came and joined us to cover the holiday shifts, he was a very strict Muslim and refused to really interact with me because I was female, he also only had been there a day when he went to management to tell them that Ion wasn't doing his job properly, this was a misunderstanding with a work sheet that was an easy mistake to make, so that really upset Ion, he was quite a sensitive guy.

I was working with Mo on a shift and I was on a break when I got a call to go to the customer services desk, I got there to be told an old lady had been scared outside by a beggar as he had stood by her car door waiting for her to get out to ask for money, I asked Mo to come with me and he said no he doesn't go outside, I said we wasn't going in the car park but just outside to see if we can see anyone, he said it's not our job and the woman should phone the police herself.

I went outside and Mo followed me shouting "it could be a set up" , I said this is our job, he said again no , so I told him to "crack on and do what you want", I told a manager what had happened and the manager confronted him and he lied and said he asked me to come and support him checking the car park but I refused and he even got on the phone to report me to Terry, thankfully the truth came out as staff heard what really happened as they was there.

Adam let it slip to Mo when they was in a conversation that I was gay, Mo went mad about it and when I came in with my partner to meet a friend in Starbucks he let his disgust show, we was sat in Starbucks and I could feel someone watching me and I turned to see Mo staring at me give me a dirty look, I tried to ignore him but five minutes later he was still staring, so I went over and said " what's your problem ?" he replied "you", I said "I'm out with friends and don't need you staring at me", he suddenly went all dramatic throwing his arms up in the air and started shouting " move away from me please move away", I shook my head and walked back to where I was sitting and Mo shouted out " you're a twat" I was so angry I tried to phone Terry but no answer, I finally spoke to Laura and told her everything and she assured me he would never be on a shift with me again, what the hell is wrong with these people, it's like they was scrapping the barrel with the guards and just hiring idiots.

It was the day before Christmas eve and I was working with Baj so I was extremely bored, I was on cctv and I noticed a male packing his shopping bags down an aisle , this was strange behaviour, but to look at the guy he was mid-fifties, tall , slim and very smartly dressed like a teacher with a suit jacket, cardigan, white shirt with it open at the top, with a neck scarf around his neck and wearing glasses, not your normal looking shoplifter , I followed him on camera around the store watching him select items and put them in the bags that was in his trolley, he then came near the front of the store and went and queued up at the kiosk, there was no point in getting Baj to help me, so I asked a manager called Dan and said to him " I think this guy is not going to pay for his shopping", we continued to watch him and he paid for a lottery ticket, then made his way out of the store, me and Dan followed the male outside when I asked him to come back in the store, I lead the way and Dan followed behind the male, we was walking back in and I thought ' oh this was a nice easy stop' then I felt the male's trolley hit me in the back , I turned to see the guy was scuffling with Dan, the guy had tried to run away but Dan had got him, I went over to assist and we pinned the guy to the floor, he calmed down and we took him out the back, not long after police came and arrested him.

Leading up to Christmas and after we was being hit by the worse shoplifter by far, he was hitting on everyone else's shift, he would select electrical items then run out of a fire door to a waiting car, so by the time the fire door alarm activated and found out what it was the guy was long gone, so far he had stolen eight hundred pounds worth in two weeks, then I was on shift with a new guy called Hussein he was a nice guy and very helpful, I went off to do a few bits and came back, I went on the cameras and checked the electrical aisle and noticed a TV was missing, so I looked back on the footage and saw the known guy picking it up, I through shit where is he?, he must still be in the store as no fire door alarms had gone off, I asked Hussein to walk around and see if there is a TV dumped anywhere while I looked on the cameras for the guy, Hussein radioed me and said he had found a trolley, I asked him to bring it back to the front of the store, he did then called me over as the guy had come over asking for his trolley with another TV in his hand , I told him we knew who he was , he tried to deny it, I took the TV off him and asked him to leave the store, that was a good team effort, there was three TV's and loads of other items in the trolley which amounted to a thousand pounds so it was a good catch.

This guy had stolen loads from us and other stores all he got was a few months inside it was a joke really, kind of fighting a losing battle but shoplifting was now seen as a very low priority, and I understand the police's decision and it's the government's fault for the cut backs.

I worked New Year's eve on the doors, Sarah was head door and I was supervisor inside, it was drum and bass music (not my favourite), to me there wasn't enough of us inside but we managed it.

 The countdown was happening and right on the bong I saw a fight break out, I pulled one of the males out into a side room, a male was jealous as he saw his ex-girlfriend kissing her new boyfriend, despite this guy had his new girlfriend with him, we managed to sort it , apart from that it went well.

At the store we had another gang that came along, they first stole five hundred pounds worth of perfume, which was missed as the relief guard was late to work, I also noticed on a walk around that there was an empty space where packs of nicotine sprays was meant to be, I got the staff to do a check on the system and my thoughts was right, twenty packs was missing and the packs was thirty pounds each, so we had lost six hundred pounds, I spent ages going through the cctv to see who it was, it was hours of footage but I managed to find the guy who had taken them, he would come in as soon as the store opened, which was the perfect time as the guards would always arrive late, I couldn't wait to catch him.

I decided to come into work the following day on my early shift so I was ready for the store to open and hopefully catch the guy.

So the next day I came in fifteen minutes early, got my morning jobs done and was waiting at the front of the store ready and waiting, the doors opened and I didn't see the male come in but did see a female who was acting strange so I followed her on camera, she went straight to the health and beauty aisle,

I saw her select a bunch of expensive razor blades and put them in her bag, I beckoned the manager over and explained what I saw, so we was waiting at the door for her, she went and paid for a cheap drink and walked out the door where I stopped her, I escorted her to the security room , she had about one hundred pounds worth of razor blades, she admitted she knew the bloke who stole the perfume and nicotine sprays , the manager wanted the police called , so we did.. We waited for ages... to the point the woman was getting on my nerves, so I sat just outside and watched her through the glass, she even fell asleep, it was four hours later when the police turned up and all they gave her was a caution, what a waste of time.

So I didn't get the guy I wanted but at least I got a catch, I spoke to our boss Terry and asked if the following day instead of working a middle shift if I could work a morning shift with Adam so we could try and catch the guy, he agreed.

We came in early before our shift started, got our radios on and planned for the catch, we waited and we didn't see the guy, it was frustrating, then suddenly Adam radioed me "quick kirst come to the front door ", he had spotted a different guy putting razor blades into his coat, we stopped him and brought him back in, items was recovered and the male was banned, we so wanted to catch the main guy, we continued to search for him, then Adam spotted another guy we wanted, the male picked up some items and walked out the door without paying, we stopped him and did the same as the last, we had a productive morning but didn't catch the guy we wanted.

The next shift was my morning shift, and guess what?... he came in, I called the manager and told him but the manager decided he wanted to deter him instead, so the guy just paid for a cheap packet of biscuits and went to leave the store when I stopped him and said to him " I know what you have been doing in here, do not come back in, if you do I will let you think you're getting away with it then I will stop you and call the police" he said ok and left, I never did see him again .

As mine and Adam's joint shift went so well we decided to do it again with our bosses permission, it wasn't long into our shift when I spotted a male down an aisle stuffing items into a carrier bag, I said to Adam "let's do the stop" (we are meant to see selection but this was too obvious to ignore), Adam got him just in time as the guy was walking out, he had two hundred pounds worth of razor blades, we called the police on this one and he was arrested, at court he was fined, I always thought this was a stupid outcome to given people who are homeless and on drugs, where do they think they're going to get the money from, yep shoplifting so it's a silly vicious circle.

Adam and I made such a good team, but things were going to take a turn for all of us.

Jason's behaviour changed dramatically which made us feel uncomfortable, he put us on edge, we felt like he was going to flip out any minute by his strange behaviour, one minute he would be talking to us then suddenly he would start running for no reason, he kept doing it, it was very strange then he started picking his nose behind the cctv podium and we would go on there and the keyboard would be covered in flakes of dried snot, we all wasn't happy about it and we tried to tell Terry but he just dismissed us, then Jason would sneeze on the monitors and leave it so there would also be dried snot stains all over the screens, we all slowly stopped using the cameras because we couldn't deal with it, then he started getting blood on our paper work, I was thinking about talking to Jason about it but it was all such an awkward and sensitive subject to mention and I didn't want to get into trouble.

Myself, Adam and Ion had a chat, we were tired not being able to go on the cctv due to Jason's bad habits, so we came up with an idea of getting some wipes and we was going to say that all of us have got to clean it down after use so we wouldn't have to clean his snot ourselves, it worked for a while then Jason kept forgetting and we had to keep reminding him.

One time he made me feel so sick I nearly had to go home, Jason went to show me a picture on his phone, I looked at it and his phone was covered in massive bits of snot stuck all over the screen (how can that not bother him?) I couldn't eat that day I was that traumatised. I asked Terry if it was possible if Jason had any mental health issues and he said there was none, how can Jason think all this was normal?

I hated having to deal with kids shoplifting, it was such a pain as you have to get an adult to collect them , one child aged around fourteen, I was watching him select a bag of sweets he then walked down the homecare aisle which is strange for a child to do but it was so he could conceal the bag of sweets in his pocket, he then went to self-scan and paid for a drink, I stopped him at the door and he tried to run, so I grabbed onto his backpack and pulled him back, we went to the security room and I got him to call his mother, the mother wanted to talk to me, she was crying down the phone and begged me not to call the police, I reassured her that I wasn't and just needed an adult to pick him up, she came to collect him and she was so angry with him saying "this is not what we do ", she explained he was hanging around with a boy who keeps shoplifting , she apologised for him and they left with the mother giving the lad an earful.

The next child I caught shoplifting was a different experience, he was only eleven, his friends said they would go and tell his dad, the lad was quite upset about being in trouble and was still crying when his dad turned up, his dad stormed in saw his son was crying and said "don't worry son you haven't done anything wrong, they are just fucking jobsworths", and stormed out of the store with his son following.

It was about nine in the morning and I was walking around the store it was quite quiet for a morning trade, I saw out the corner of my eye a guy with a high-visual vest on marching quickly up the alcohol aisle , I thought this was a bit strange, so I quickly went on the cctv podium and saw the male select loads of expensive alcohol, I phoned for a manager and two managers came and joined me at the front of the store by the podium, still watching the male, he then went and picked up some tin foil, he opened the packet and was tearing off the foil and placing it around the security alarm tags on the bottle (it stops the alarm from working at the door) we kept watching him and he was putting the bottles in a fabric bag, he then dumped the empty basket at the till and walked out the front door, I stopped him and grabbed his arm and he said "na I don't think so ", and tried to get away from me, me and the two managers pinned him to the floor, I shouted for a member of staff to call the police, the male was still trying to throw himself about, he was really strong, he tried to spit at me and I pushed his head against the floor (worse thing is being spat at) he was constantly throwing abuse at us and laughing and even said all his going to get is a slap on the wrist for it, well I thought that might be the case but it seemed he was let out of prison early so he was sent back to prison for the remainder of his sentence which was about nine months, the items was recovered and was about four hundred pounds worth, so It was a great stop even though it was hard work, but people on drugs are desperate.

We had this old guy that staff was suspicious about , they told me he would linger about near the magazine and football stickers but didn't see him with anything , so I watched him the following day, he came in and picked up a basket , went to the magazines and I saw him pick up a load of football stickers I watched him walk up an aisle and he put the stickers in his coat pocket, he selected a few items and put it in his basket and went and paid for those items but not the stickers , we stopped him outside and he was angry straight away, we went to the office and he demanded to speak to the manager so mike came and we explained everything, mike hated shoplifters , so we went in and the guy was saying he didn't want the stickers getting damaged and that's why he put it in his pocket and not the basket and he had simply forgotten , mike looked at him and his look showed he didn't believe what he said and said he would be banned, the bloke jumped up and got in mikes face shouting " you calling me a shoplifter" mike replied " that's exactly what I am saying " , I really thought a fight was about to kick off, he said he was going to appeal it but it never happened, I had to ask him to leave the store a few weeks later, he said that he had got a letter from the head store saying that his banning was lifted, I told him unless he brings that letter and shows us we wouldn't be letting him back in, he never did show us or come back into the store, I've seen him a few times out and about and he gives me dirty looks, it makes me laugh , you're the thief mate not me .

One of my favourite times when I had to restrain a shop lifter was when one day I was on the cctv and saw this guy with a back pack and carrier bag down the beauty aisle , he was rummaging in his carrier bag, he then reached up , took a load of razor blades off the hanger and put them in his carrier bag , I was on my own, there was no other security officer in and no managers that I know would come and help, I spotted the back door man (that would often tell me stories about how hard he was) I asked him to help do the stop and he told me he can't , I didn't have time to discuss this as the guy was walking out the door , he saw me , went back in and was going out the other exit , I grabbed his back pack (always a good way to grab someone when you have hold of the straps , harder for them to get away) it started to slide off his shoulders so I grabbed his arm and swung him round and pushed him into the kitchen roll stand that was at the front of the store so I could knock him off balance and regain control of him , so it was a soft landing into the kitchen rolls , quick thinking for me , when he went down I could grab both his arms and put them in a lock , I told him to calm down and to come with me and he did , he said something quite nice , he said I had a reputation for catching people and if he had saw me he wouldn't of bothered trying , in his bag he had over £200 worth of razor blades so I called the police and as he was wanted for another shop lifting incident elsewhere the police came and arrested him.

The most obvious one I spotted, was where I was coming out of the staff area onto the shop floor this male was walking past me while opening a box containing an aerial booster, he went down a aisle near a member of staff and hid behind one of the cages, I could still see through part of the cage as he took the item out of the box , and put it inside his coat and dumped the box on the shelve , I don't think I ever had such a easy catch then that one, it must have been quite embarrassing for him as when I was waiting for him at the front doors, he bumped into someone he knew and was chatting for a few minutes then I stopped , it was worth about £35 , we just banned him and escorted him out .

Now I'm going to tell you something I shouldn't really, us security have to follow a code called A.S.C.O.N.E, which stands for approach , selection, concealment, no-payment and exit, I didn't always follow that code but I was always careful, but you should be 100 per cent sure so despite seeing that I was always sure, but I know some guards would do it on a wim without anything and that annoys me , I nearly made a complaint at asdas once, we had done our shopping and was pushing our trolley out when the alarm went off, this guard jumped and I mean jumped in front of our trolley, I said to him it was most likely our razors as that's the only thing that had a security tag on it but he proceeded to go through all our bags like we was a shoplifter , everyone was looking and I felt embarrassed as I still a guard at the store down the road, because I knew some of the guards there I just messaged them saying I wasn't happy with how he dealt with it , if I had been at another store and that happened I would of kicked off, I don't mind them checking as they have a job to do , but technically I don't have to allow it , I had paid for my items , and he should follow " ascone", now if he had just approached me normally I wouldn't of minded but jumping in front of our trolley and holding onto the trolley so we couldn't go made it look like we had done something wrong, I didn't even treat my real shoplifters like that, I made sure embarrassment was at a minimum unless there behaviour meant there was no way of keeping it like that.

I would approach the person and ask them politely to come back into the store , 9 times out of 10 they would , and other times yes there was a bit of scene because there trying to get away with a lot of stuff and would refuse to come back in.

Things was changing strangely on the doors, I had been training new staff for nearly two years now, I believed I would get something out of it and I had already been asked during the meeting to be a trainer then I heard some other door staff had been sent on a training course to be an official SIA trainer and I wasn't asked, that was a real kick in the teeth I was fuming.

So this confused me, they was happy for me to train people with no extra pay, they asked me in the meeting to be a trainer, they never mentioned anyone else, yet I had been kept off this course, this really knocked my confidence, no-one even spoke to me about it, I just went and spoke to Sarah about it all.

Then the shock came that Aaron was selling his share of the company to Nick and was leaving, I had some major issues with him, but I learnt to respect him in the end, he wasn't two faced and always spoke honestly.

After Aaron left Helen's shifts suddenly dropped dramatically and now only had three shifts at the club, she asked Nick and he said he would sort it, but nothing happened, then Harry from the doors took over the rota (Aaron used to sort out the rotas) and Helen would message for shifts and he would just ignore her so Helen started looking for another job.

Helen got a great full – time job and was due to leave the company and start her training in two months' time, so I needed to make a choice for our relationship, if I kept doing both jobs we wouldn't see each other, so I spoke to Terry to see if I could possible go part – time at the store to which he said I could, so I was thinking of going part-time there and still do the doors, so that is what my plan was.

But things started taking the piss , two new girls who had just done their badges was under me to be trained, as Helen was now leaving we needed to train one of them to take over from her on the front door, but the girl we choose called Lisa to do that wasn't getting the shifts, instead a female called Bex was getting the shifts (because she was good friends with Harry) this didn't help us when we needed to train Lisa for the sake of the club, it was like favouritism again, favouritism over looking after a contract, that made sense.

I still hadn't heard from the office about anything with me doing any training and it had been over a month now , then one night Sarah got injured at the club while restraining a male, they fell to the floor and the males elbow went into Sarah's ribs, she was in a lot of pain and at the end of the night me and Helen took her to the hospital, Nick met us up there, he always went to the hospital if one of the door staff was injured (which was really nice of him).

Helen went down to x-ray with Sarah for support and me and Nick went out for a cigarette, this was the first time he mentioned the training and he said I would be on the next one, I didn't believe him to be honest as they had just trained up five people they certainly wouldn't need any more for their sister company (training company) I believed I was just being strung along, with that and Helen not being given anymore shifts, where a few others had six days a week, along with them not caring about someone needing to be trained up for the front door at the club for when Helen leaves pushed me to the point of making changes.

I was starting to feel like how I did before even though I knew I was good at training people (honestly not being big headed) and they probably knew I was but because yet again I didn't have the right look and that was probably the reason, but if it was, why couldn't they be honest with me, I really wanted this I would have tried to change if it meant I could do the training too.

Sometime later I got a text message from Bex, asking if I had an issue with her being on the course, it seemed someone had overheard a conversation I had had and went back to Bex about it, so I called her, I explained what had been said, I was not slagging her off as a person or as a door supervisor, I just didn't understand why when she had been only doing door work for two years, against me with seventeen years and had already been training people for two years, I wasn't saying she shouldn't be on it, but you get what I am mean, someone is quick to shit stir, I relayed to her that Nick had said it was a short notice thing (the training course) and didn't ask me because he didn't think I would be able to get the time off my day job, Bex replied "no it wasn't short notice we had known for months" (now it was Bex shit stirring and putting thoughts in my head, I didn't realise at the time but I was being manipulated by her).

Chapter 7

She had also heard about us talking about her getting more shifts, again it wasn't about her as a person , it was the fact Helen was asking for one more shift and Bex had six shifts and a new guy who had just got his badge was on six as well, the conversation wasn't about them they was just used as an example, Helen had mentioned that she needed to look for another job as she wasn't getting any more than three shifts, someone else said "maybe they haven't got any to offer" which was when Bex and two other people's names was mentioned as they all had six shifts, meaning there was enough shifts, again it was just names being used as an example not slagging them off.

We also spoke about that a female needed to be trained at the club to take over Helen's place, to which Bex replied "look I am getting more shifts because I'm friends with Harry that's just the way it is and I don't really care about anyone being trained at the club it's not my problem" the arrogance of her was a joke so I just ended the chat.

That really pissed me off, so it was now going to be like that, I spoke to Helen and decided to quit when she leaves and just stay full-time at the store and study to progress in my own way, I wasn't going to be used which I felt like I was and now what Bex had said made me realise it even more.

I was already starting to feel ill I didn't need the stress and games that was going on, I can't explain how I felt ill, I kept feeling spaced out like the feeling you get before you go dizzy and pass out, so I was really starting to struggle with that and all this crap that was happening.

So when I was at the club I started to train Michael to take over from me when I left, I was doing it for the club and Sarah , the company couldn't careless, so I was spending a lot of time with Michael and training him and I also would take a step back and would watch him take over to see if there was anything that needed improving on, also at this time I kept feeling like I was going to have a panic attack or something so I tried to stay near to Helen and Sarah, as I knew if anything happened to me I would be in safe hands with them.

Michael was smashing it, for his age and experience he was a great supervisor, I was very proud of him he had worked so hard, a great guy with a good head on his shoulders, he will go far in life.

Sarah was such great support, I couldn't wish for a better friend, she's one of those rare people that are loyal to the core and would always be there for you, she did try and talk me out of leaving, but I felt so hurt and used.

it was nearly two months on and I still hadn't heard from the office about training, I was tired of being used and here I was built up only to be pulled back down again, did I think I was some of the problem, of course, but I'm not the kind of person to go swanning in the office and say "what's going on?", I feared the rejection, I've always been rejected why would I welcome it, I felt if I wasn't good enough then I would leave, they knew I was leaving and didn't bother to talk to me about it so to me that speaks volumes.

So it came to mine and Helen's last shift, it didn't feel real, Nick and the office manager Jodie came up to say goodbye to us, Nick gave me a hug and didn't say much, Jodie spoke to me for a bit but I wasn't interested as I knew she had lied and told something totally untrue to the club about why I decided to leave, I felt very let down by her, I thought a lot of her and she made something up so the company didn't look bad.

The door company gave us some lovely flowers and cards, the club team got us tie clips, flowers and lots of chocolates, even the club got us personalised hoodies and cups , it was so nice and felt very loved, I took a few pictures of inside the club as memories because I knew I wouldn't be back, all in all I had spent ten years at the club on and off, so it was a big part of my life, the last thing I did was switch off the club's sign and that was it.

So that was it, the dream I had in my head was over, all the years of fighting to prove my worth had been stripped away by this company that built me up, they had destroyed me, Helen had left the following week to go away for her three week training for her new job, I was so proud of her but felt like I was being left behind a bit, she was going onto a job to be proud of, I felt like I had been let down in a big way by the company, the company that made me believe in door family , that made me trust them and because of my past I found it hard to trust people, I spiralled out of control but didn't allow Helen to know, I didn't want it to affect her training for her new job, in secret I went to the doctors and was put back on the anti-depressants.

So I became a recluse for a while, friends messaged me and I ignored them, not meaning to be rude but I didn't want to talk to anyone, I went inside myself, I kept thinking where did I go wrong ?, I was always nice, honest, trustworthy and would give my job a hundred per cent sometimes even more, but it's never enough, I was always being fucked over somehow, and over taken by really nasty vindictive, manipulative people, who wasn't even that good at the job, I guess nice people do finish last.

I had time to reflect and just think it is what it is and I tried to contact Nick but he ignored me, a few months past and I contacted him and I received back the most nasty lying text message, I can only think people love to gossip and make things up about people or what he messaged me he had made it up himself to pass the guilt, apparently I posted things on Facebook and instagram slagging the company off, I know I never did that and I am not the kind of person to do that, I'm more of the kind of person that thinks ' show them what they're missing' so that angered me, after everything I did for them , instead of admitting guilt or just ignore what has happened he decided to shift the blame onto me, it just shows it's not me as every company or managers I've had, I've left on good terms and could go back to them at any time, apart from that company, so that shows the truth of it.

so is anything the truth , well I never put anything about them on any social media sites that's a lie, did I slag any of them off well I guess I did but all I said was the truth , about how I was treated, about how downhill it has gone, yep it was the truth, spoke about how the owner was a hypocrite .. he would say he was dead against drugs yet one of his staff constantly takes steroids, ok it's a different kind of drug and I'm not slagging everyone off that takes it but this particular person has made himself seriously ill and keeps losing his temper and had assaulted many customers, how he's got away with it I don't know, but for the years I was there it was drummed into us , customer service , customer service , that we wouldn't lose our tempers like other companies then allowing this to constantly happen, and the only other person I have spoken about is Bex and that she's a nasty bit of work, even most of the staff still there cannot stand her and the way she speaks to people again another one that kept having complaints about how rude she is yet now part of management .

At least I've never been two faced like some of them , like Bex, Nick and Nicole.

I want to say that no company is perfect there is always something in most places , but you can't be fake and make out your something when you are not.

Would I ever work for the company again , not in a million years , the good times are gone its controlled but nasty people now, you can join if you do everything they say and tell them how wonderful they are, if you don't do that you haven't got a chance.
Would I ever talk to the owner again, not in a fucking million years, normally I don't hold grudges , life is to short, but liars and assholes don't deserve my time If he ever tried to talk to me I would blank him, sound petty ..if only you knew everything they had done , he had a chance to sort it and he didn't bother he decided to believe people that was telling him lies for there own gratification.

Do I think about it much , not really not anymore, I have so much going on now , writing books , new career , me and Helen having more time and money to have days out , as me and Sarah have said they have done us a favour and if I had to I would say, thank you for treating me like shit because my life is so much better now I have left your company , was fucking horrible at the time, but I truly think everything happens for a reason, and even though I didn't get to do what I wanted to do in door work , I think I came close to it , so im happy with that.
I'm a stronger person for it, I have spent over the years getting knocked down, lied to , spoken to like shit, used etc. etc., I'm done feeling sad about it, I'm more confidant (which I thought I never would be) I speak out, I know my worth, fuck image, I live by the same principles , still have my morals and I won't let anyone drag me down again, I've conquered so many demons in my life I won't let this affect me anymore.

To anyone reading this who maybe going through a time of self-doubt or depression, every single one of us are worth a lot, it doesn't matter what job we do or how much money we earn, we are all the same, same feelings everything, everyone should be treated with worth and respect, we are all human and it's what I live by.

It was so nice not doing the doors, I missed the team but Helen and i got to do things at the weekend that we couldn't do before as we were always committed to regular door shifts.

I was less tired at my day job now and I had a plan and I was going to stick to it, then shocker, four months on the store and all the other stores under the same name was cutting back hugely on security staff, so we were told we could be made redundant.

So hearing this wasn't great news but to be honest I think I had had enough of the store due to all the useless guards I kept working with and the stress of it all , Adam was the only one that kept me sane there.

Everyone is trying to save money no matter what, whether it be by charging more money or making staff cut backs , which I understand to a point but it seems people are not willing to make a effort to try and make more money, I'm talking about clubs, pubs and shopping stores, coming up with ideas to get more customers . so let's talk about staff cut backs that keeps happening , it will get to the point when they can't cut anymore staff then what do they do then ? , the thing I think is the better the customer service the more people will continue to go there, as myself shopping wise I mainly got to m&s , yes it's a bit dear but the food quality is amazing, the stores are clean and tidy, staff are so helpful and friendly , toilets are spotless .

The store I worked at, most of the staff are lovely and friendly but are under pressure and stressed, the younger staff are rude, bored and can't be bothered.

The store is not that clean as no-one is keeping an eye on the cleaners as most of them spend their shift in the canteen and only come out if they get called for a spillage, the toilets are disgusting and out of date, some of the managers don't give a crap.

They have cut the staff back so much that when the tills are busy all the floor staff end up going on the tills so there is no one left to answer customer questions or deter shop lifters, so that's when I was there, from what I've seen over 10 months since I've left it's gotten so much worse, the hard working team leaders are gone, these people picked up the slack when lazy managers couldn't be bother , they went from 4 security guards to one , and went from 174 guarding hours to around 54, they have cut the cleaning staff, the place is dirty and not a nice atmosphere I would hate to think what the theft lose is now.

Not long after I started we got a count of around 60 thousand pounds on theft for the year, with our hard work we got it down to 35 thousand pounds , now they hardly have a guard I dread to think what there next count will be , I'suddeve had staff members telling me that people are just walking out with alcohol then coming back later and stealing more, the staff shouldn't put themselves at risk , if the store believe they are saving money with these cut backs when they lose more the following year what are they going to do then? They don't care about staff like they say, when us officers knew we was being made redundant , it got around what hours the remaining guard would be doing and people were concerned that there wouldn't be a guard on in the evening and that's when you get a lot of people kicking off or drunk people coming in , how's the staff meant to handle it ? it's not their job, there job is to serve people.

 So after finding out I could be made redundant I started to think that it might be a good thing, to find something new as I got to the point when the other guards was on I went and sat out the back watching the cctv from there, I used to spot shoplifters on the cameras there and run out and catch them and the guard on the cameras at the front of the store wouldn't even notice, I was getting so fed up and a bit lazy as I couldn't be bothered anymore, no one cared if you did well at the job (I'm not including staff at the store in that statement as they was thankful), but the other guards did sod all everyday so I thought as I was being made redundant I would do the same (I know I shouldn't have thought like that but I did).

I was still catching a lot of shoplifters, a catch would always cheer me up and when I got to work with Adam, but Adam knew he wouldn't get to stay or get redundancy money so he left and got another job closer to where he lived, I was gutted to see him go but we all had to move on anyway, so the last few weeks I worked there without Adam was hard but I got through it.

I had a feeling I would be one of the people that would get made redundant, basically they had to get rid of over half of the guards they had so I was competing with a lot of guards for very few jobs and there was loads of guards who had been with the company a lot longer than me, so I kind of knew.

I spoke to our manager and asked if it was rated on performance, he said no , so I said to him " you could end up with a load of useless guards?" , he replied yes , what a joke ..

So I was made redundant with a 6 weeks redundancy pay which wasn't to bad

I have enjoyed being in this industry but I do hope to get out of it at some point, it is a thankless job, I would say 70 percent of people look down at security , I don't know if that's through bad experience or they have seen lazy officers, but I don't think people relise how much some of us do work, and I would always try my hardest for people , I'm never rude , but I do get treated like shit sometimes, but if something serious happened they would look to us to deal with it.

Also being female you get a lot of hatred , and even more so now with different ethnic races, so let's go back to talking about race, I do not condone any type of hate, but I've had it done to me.

I remember one night on the doors I had a male standing on a low wall inside and told him to get down, he did the first time then got back up again, I told him again, he ignored me and kept ignoring me , so I called over a colleague and we got him down and took him to the incident room, head door Sarah came in and we asked him why he ignored what I had said to him, he explained that in his country women do not tell men what to do , and that is still his way and he will not change and that we have to expect that and learn that we have to get males to deal with him and not females, this angered me , I've never had this , maybe a guy would say I would rather speak to a male , which is fine but to be told that he would not expect being told what to do by a female was very offence, we called the club manager in who was the same nationality as the guy, the guy said to him " you know what I mean brother " the manager was furious about this and said " I am not your brother and do not disrespect these ladies " , he was asked to leave for the rest of the night, I never saw him again thankfully .

People will push you and test you thinking that being female is weak, but people soon relise not all of us are.

When I worked at the store I got on well with most of the staff and only a few managers the rest of them looked down on us.
I never understand this whole looking down on people, no matter what job we do we all make a difference and we are all needed, it winds me up sometimes people acting like they are better then others, am I guilty of that ...not with working people no, only those who live there life on the dole because they don't work and don't want to work, I think they are worse than drug addicts, I have a lot of time for them , as most of them have gone through such a hard life , worse that we can ever imagine .

Sometimes now I still spot some and we always say hello to each other , people I'm with are shocked and ask if we are friends or how do I know them, they are human like us , I had a good report with some shoplifters, probably because I respect them and didn't treat them like shit like some (maybe hence the bad experience with security staff)

I got some lovely leaving gifts from the people at the store; I was going to really miss them they were a great bunch of people.

I later saw Baj working in the store I can't believe he got kept on , but to be honest our manager didn't care about performance or complaints as long as that person turned up for there shifts , so even thou I was a bit sad, I was glad to be leaving the stress of him and the store behind

So i left and went back to an old door company I used to work for , it wasn't what I wanted to do but it was something for now.

I heard a lot of bad stuff about the door company I left , Bex had brown nosed her way into management I was really shocked not because I disliked her but because she wasn't good at her job and was now part of management , she couldn't use a radio properly, she couldn't cope with stress and would have to go and have a cry somewhere, she was rude to other staff and customers yet had made her way up, it's amazing how some people who are false manage to do that, but she was opposite to what the company use to stand for, they used to pride themselves on customer service and looking after their staff and now that was all thrown out the window .

There was an event that Sarah used to be in charge of and she always dealt with it well, this year Bex was in charge while there was no issues the staff wasn't looked after, they had no breaks , and Bex didn't bother in making sure staff had water as it was a hot day, she just sat in the management tent for the whole shift and didn't bother checking the staff was ok, quite a few staff was really pissed off and one of them told me they had to ask the event staff for some water as Bex didn't bother, a few of them said they wouldn't work any events again for them after that, it's a shame because events was always good with them but it sounds like they are turning into the security company I worked for before I joined them, the company they always used to take the piss out off.

Most events was always hard and stressful and most was long so just the little things of quick breaks, water etc would mean a lot and for the higher management to allow Bex not to look after the staff is shocking I never thought they would start behaving like that.

I would hear about the staff acting badly , assaulting customers, being arrogant and rude to other staff, it was never like that and I look back and feel sad about how badly it has changed because up until about 4 months before I left it was so great , apart from a few incidents but no company is perfect, but I loved what the company had stood for , I enjoyed going that bit extra for customers, that I didn't have to turn a blind eye to door staff assaulting people , I was proud to work for them but now I hear they have a bad reputation.

They put in place that door staff that was friends with each other outside of work wasn't allowed to work with each other and they started pulling people from venues for it, yet Bex's partner Dan who ran a venue was allowed to socialize with his team, that makes sense doesn't it? It's like they just did it for a power trip .

And management wonder why some decent door staff was leaving because of it all, well I say wonder they didn't wonder they would just decide that the people leaving were traitors , they just can't see what really it going on, a few door staff that I'm still friends with are leaving because of the way they have been treated mainly by Bex but I'm sure she made up lies about it, but the truth will come out in the end it always does.

If anyone should have gone up to management it should have been Sarah, one of the very few best head doorman I have ever worked with, a real leader, always looked after her staff, didn't throw her weight about she is very humble and everyone liked and respected her unlike Bex, so management started treating Sarah like crap and cutting her hours, so she started looking for another job and got one , a job with career prospects, good money and great pension something she didn't have with the door company, I'm sure management will say she betrayed them rather than the truth that their behaviour gave her the push to get a great career, and as a friend I'm so proud of her she really deserves it she gave the door company everything , she devoted herself to them, lost relationships for them , her free time and they repaid her by treating her like crap.
So now the last bit about me, as the saying goes everything happens for a reason, it really does after working for many security companies , some better then others, working long shifts and being messed about, I have now got a full-time job, a job that's classed as a respected job, with good prospects , great pension , more me time, time to write my books , it means a lot to me, its not to much to ask for is it ?

12015488R00066

Printed in Germany
by Amazon Distribution
GmbH, Leipzig